**Books are to be returned on or before
the last date below.**

8/01

WITHDRAWN 20/11/19

LIBREX —

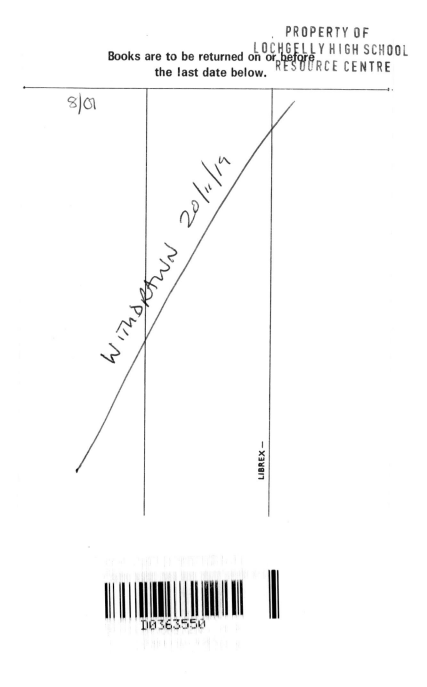

Heinemann Educational Publishers
Halley Court, Jordan Hill, Oxford OX2 8EJ
A division of Reed Educational & Professional Publishing Ltd

OXFORD   MELBOURNE   AUCKLAND
JOHANNESBURG   BLANTYRE   GABORONE
IBADAN   PORTSMOUTH (NH) USA   CHICAGO

04 03 02 01
10 9 8 7 6 5 4 3 2

ISBN 0 435 125230

Cover design by The Point
Cover photographs: Passengers embarking onto Queen Mary on her maiden
voyage, 1936, Hulton Getty (04066157 or 12982978); Tri-star jet landing,
Sunset ACE Photo Agency (AA/0364GK)
Photographs: J. Allan Cash, p.18; Robert Harding, p.61; J. Allan Cash, p.64;
Photodisc, p.107; Tap Richards, p.121; The Art Archive, p.162;
Associated Press, p.182.
Typeset by Tek-Art, Croydon, Surrey
Printed and bound in the United Kingdom by Clays Ltd, St Ives plc

FROM HERE
TO THERE

A NEW WINDMILL BOOK
OF TRAVEL WRITING

**Edited by Steve Barlow and
Steve Skidmore**

Heinemann
New Windmills

Heinemann Educational Publishers
Halley Court, Jordan Hill, Oxford OX2 8EJ
A division of Reed Educational & Professional Publishing Ltd

OXFORD   MELBOURNE   AUCKLAND
JOHANNESBURG   BLANTYRE   GABORONE
IBADAN   PORTSMOUTH (NH) USA   CHICAGO

04 03 02 01
10 9 8 7 6 5 4 3 2

ISBN 0 435 125230

Cover design by The Point
Cover photographs: Passengers embarking onto Queen Mary on her maiden
voyage, 1936, Hulton Getty (04066157 or 12982978); Tri-star jet landing,
Sunset ACE Photo Agency (AA/0364GK)
Photographs: J. Allan Cash, p.18; Robert Harding, p.61; J. Allan Cash, p.64;
Photodisc, p.107; Tap Richards, p.121; The Art Archive, p.162;
Associated Press, p.182.
Typeset by ⚘ Tek-Art, Croydon, Surrey
Printed and bound in the United Kingdom by Clays Ltd, St Ives plc

Contents

Introduction for teachers

This anthology is intended to help resource the National Curriculum requirement for studying non-fiction texts. In combining a mixture of extracts by authors suggested in the National Curriculum with material which is often ephemeral, occasionally offbeat and sometimes macabre, we have aimed to produce a thought-provoking and user-friendly collection to capture students' imagination and allow for study of different styles of literary and non-literary travel writing at different periods in time.

Activities are provided for every extract in the book, though whether all sections, or all extracts in a section are covered will obviously depend on time available and the wishes of the individual user. We have therefore tried to make the activities format flexible so that any number of activities may be pursued in any order.

Each section ends with an activity intended to draw the student's attention to a comparison between extracts and advice on further reading: and the book ends with a project section aimed at encouraging a creative response to the material.

We hope that you will find in this collection sufficient material to convince your students that reading a good travel writer is almost as interesting as travelling – and a lot more comfortable!

Steve Barlow and *Steve Skidmore*

Introduction for students

People write about their travels for many reasons such as:

- to help readers understand countries and people that they may never visit

- to give advice

- to tell people about their adventures

- to sell holidays.

Samuel Johnson wrote the first Dictionary of the English Language. Nearly two hundred and fifty years ago, this is what he had to say about travelling:

All travel has its advantages. If the passenger visits better countries, he may learn to improve his own, and if fortune carries him to worse, he may learn to enjoy it.

You have often heard me complain of finding myself disappointed by books of travels; I am afraid travel itself will end likewise in disappointment. One town, one country, is very like another . . . a traveller seldom stays long enough to investigate and compare . . .

Books of travels will be good in proportion to what a man has previously in his mind; his knowing what to observe; his power of contrasting one mode of life with another. As the Spanish proverb says, 'He, who would bring home the wealth of the Indies, must carry the wealth of the Indies with him.'

Samuel Johnson (1709–1784)

Nearer our own time, Bill Bryson describes his arrival in Luxembourg on his first visit to Europe. He gives an account of the moment when the traveller realises that he is not at home any more:

> I felt like someone stepping out of doors for the first time. It was all so different: the language, the money, the cars, the number plates on the cars, the bread, the food, the newspapers, the parks, the people. And the people – why, they were Luxembourgers. I don't know why this amazed me so, but it did. I kept thinking, That man over there, he's a Luxembourger. And so is that girl. They don't know anything about the New York Yankees, they don't know the theme tune to *The Mickey Mouse Club*, they are from another world. It was just wonderful.
>
> *Bill Bryson*

Some of the extracts in this book are funny. Some are sad. Some are easy to read. Some may take a bit more effort. Some of the extracts are about discovering unexpected things about different lands and people. But many are about how, in going to see different lands and different people, the writers discover unexpected things about themselves.

Steve Barlow and *Steve Skidmore*

Section 1
Dangerous Journeys

Travelling wasn't always as safe as it is now. Journeys we now take for granted were very difficult in earlier times. But today's traveller can still find journeys that are difficult and taxing . . .

An unexpected ducking
from Operation Raleigh:
The Start of an Adventure
by John Blashford-Snell

Operation Raleigh is a project involving young people from many countries: its aim is to bring together young people from developed countries, and set them to work on projects that will be of help to poorer nations.

In Peru, one group of Venturers nearly came to grief in the swirling waters of the Tambopata River.

It was the last time that Pam Gaffin, the tall globe-trotting American, would make the river trip to Puerto Maldonado. After three months in the Peruvian rainforest, her ten-strong team had piled the unstable ***peki-peki*** with rucksacks, rations and tents for the four-hour journey on the flooded Tambopata. As they climbed aboard, the

---

peki-peki: locally built motorboat, so called because of the noise it makes.

muddy torrent hissed past, tossing huge logs like matchsticks in the spinning eddies. John, the boat's owner, pulled the toggle and the faithful Mariner outboard roared confidently. The frail craft swung out into the stream and soon they were absorbing the beauty of the emerald forest. No one spoke; all were sad to be leaving, even if it did mean going home.

Mother Nature gave them an unforgettable send-off, a magnificent sunset complete with sound effects from birds, insects and monkeys. The mighty river, now five hundred yards wide, pushed them on, its everchanging currents and whirlpools tugging at the hull. 'We sat enthralled,' recalls Pam, 'cameras clicking; but as the orange and red of the sky faded, darkness was suddenly upon us.' In fact, it was pitch black and they still had forty-five minutes to go.

Squatting in the now silent boat, the bow lookout swung a torch and strained eyes to differentiate between the shadows of swirling water and logs, or worse. 'Log! Go right!' 'Log! Go left!' came the warnings, and John swung the tiller. For a while all was well and a nervous calm descended on the crew. Suddenly came the scream 'Rock!' There was no time to react. With a splintering crash the *peki-peki* ran head-on into a great black slab that had appeared from nowhere. Water poured over the gunwales and people grabbed what they could as the craft went over.

'Everyone OK?' 'How far is the bank?' 'Stay with the boat!' 'Where's the boat?' 'Don't panic!' came the yells.

Pam thought: 'Oh my God, where are the **cayman**, the piranhas and the huge **anacondas**?' Her clothes weighed her down and it became impossible to make headway against the powerful stream. She heard John's voice crying 'I can't swim!' Nearly choked by the silt-laden water, she used her last ounce of strength to reach the dark shadow

---

cayman: South American cousin of the alligator
anaconda: large snake, a constrictor (it kills its prey by crushing it)

that was being swept along nearby, and there found six Venturers plus a half-drowned John clinging desperately to the *peki-peki*'s hull.

There was no sign of the other four, but soon they heard Kerry yelling that she was on the rock they'd hit and was staying there. Then came the faint cries of Martin and Margaret shouting from near the bank, and lastly they heard Jacqui, fighting with all the power she could muster to reach them. Her heavy hiking boots threatened to pull her down but she clung to her rucksack, which acted as a float. No one could help her – it was all that they could do to hold onto the boat that was trapped in a huge, slow-moving whirlpool, and stop it flipping again, when it would surely fill completely with water and sink.

Margaret's yells got weaker and weaker, then they stopped altogether. But now they heard that Martin was on the shore, looking for her. Jacqui was swept into the whirlpool and after a few circles she reached the survivors, totally exhausted, unable to speak. An attempt to swim the *peki-peki* to the nearest bank, three hundred yards away, proved futile, and now the cold was becoming a problem. They shivered and shook, knowing they must get out soon to avoid hypothermia. Then there came the unmistakable noise of a motor.

Sound travels far over water and it was a good four minutes before the boat appeared. They yelled and screamed like banshees – to no avail: clearly the boatman couldn't hear them above the noise of the engine. Suddenly Sara realised she had managed to hang on to the torch and amazingly it still worked. Now she flashed it at the oncoming craft but to their horror it veered away, giving them a wide berth. Then, just as they were beginning to give up hope, it turned and came slowly towards them. Its occupants were none too happy about picking strange people out of a river known to be well populated with drug smugglers, and it took an offer of twenty dollars and six gallons of petrol before they'd agree to rescue everyone. And even now the team's troubles were not over. The river currents were too tricky for the small boat to collect them all at once, so the group on the *peki-peki* was deposited on a small mud ledge sticking out from a cliff. Here they huddled, shivering and wondering if they'd ever be found again, as the ledge crumbled piece by piece into the racing water.

Kerry Kingston, the girl from Bedfordshire, was still on her rock, singing disco songs to keep her spirits up when the rescuers arrived, and eventually the Peruvians found Martin and Margaret too. No one was badly hurt, though Margaret had been rather battered when landing on the stony bank – but they were all pretty shocked. After more negotiations, their rescuers agreed to search for John's *peki-peki* and their gear, and surprisingly found a fair amount of it, plus the boat. Two and a half hours after the accident, the **Venturers** were on their way again, still shivering but singing as the tropical moon rose over Puerto Maldonado. Whilst they unloaded what kit they had left and thanked their rescuers, Liz ran up to the town to get transport. Afterwards Pam wrote: 'Standing ankle-deep in the mud, we looked up and saw the cavalry coming. Winding down the hill, headlights blazing, horns beeping, came ten moped taxis.'

As they entered the little hotel lobby, dripping wet, cold and exhausted, Venturers who'd arrived earlier saw them and without a word dashed into action. Hot kebabs were thrust into their hands and as they were herded through the courtyard to their rooms for baths, a blizzard of clothing hit them as their friends on the balcony tossed down dry t-shirts, pants, socks and shoes. 'This is what Operation Raleigh is all about,' thought Pam. 'People coping with adversity and the value of friendship.'

Venturers: volunteer workers with Operation Raleigh

The flight over the South Pole (1929)

from Exploring with Byrd
by Richard Byrd (1888–1957)

Richard Byrd was a famous American aviator. In 1926 he flew over the North Pole. He knew that if anything went wrong, there would be little possibility of rescue.

Three years later, in 1929, Byrd took his plane to the opposite end of the earth – the South Pole.

[28 November]. It was an awesome thing, creeping (so it seemed) through the narrow pass, with the black walls of Nansen and Fisher on either side, higher than the level of the wings, and watching the nose of the ship [i.e. the aeroplane] bob up and down across the face of that chunk of rock. It would move up, then slide down. Then move up, and fall off again. For perhaps a minute or two we deferred the decision; but there was no escaping it. If we were to risk a passage through the pass, we needed greater manoeuvrability than we had at that moment. Once we entered the pass, there would be no retreat. It offered no room for turn. If power was lost momentarily or if the air became excessively rough, we could only go ahead, or down. We had to climb, and there was only one way in which we could climb.

June, anticipating the command, already had his hand on the dump valve of the main tank. A pressure of the fingers – that was all that was necessary – and in two minutes 600 gallons of gasoline would gush out. I signalled to wait. Balchen held to the climb almost to the edge of a stall. But it was clear to both of us that he could not hold it long enough. Balchen began to yell and gesticulate, and it was hard to catch the words in the roar of the engines echoing from the cliffs on either side. But the meaning was manifest. 'Overboard – overboard – 200 pounds!'

Which would it be – gasoline or food? If gasoline, I thought, we might as well stop there and turn back. We could never get back to the base from the Pole. If food, the lives of all of us would be jeopardised in the event of a forced landing. Was that fair to McKinley, Balchen and June? It really took only a moment to reach the decision. The Pole, after all, was our objective. I knew the character of the three men. McKinley, in fact, had already hauled one of the food bags to the trapdoor. It weighed 125 pounds. The brown bag was pushed out and fell, spinning, to the glacier. The improvement in the flying qualities of the plane was noticeable. It took another breath and resumed the climb.

Now the down-currents over Nansen became stronger. The plane trembled and rose and fell, as if struck bodily. We veered a trifle to the right, searching for helpful rising eddies. Balchen was flying shrewdly. He maintained flight at a sufficient distance below the absolute ceiling of the plane to retain at all times enough manoeuvrability to make him master of the ship. But he was hard-pressed by circumstances; and I realised that, unless the plane was further lightened, the final thrust might bring us perilously close to the end of our reserve.

'More,' Bernt shouted. 'Another bag.'

McKinley shoved a second bag through the trapdoor, and this time we saw it hit the glacier, and scatter in a soundless explosion. Two hundred and fifty pounds of food – enough to feed four men for a month – lay strewn on the barren ice. The sacrifice swung the scales. The plane literally rose with a jump; the engines dug in, and we soon showed a gain in altitude of from 300 to 400ft. It was what we wanted. We should clear the pass with about

500 ft to spare. Balchen gave a shout of joy. It was just as well. We could dump no more food. There was nothing left to dump except McKinley's camera. I am sure that, had he been asked to put it overboard, he would have done so instantly; and I am equally sure he would have followed the precious instrument with his own body . . .

At six minutes after one o'clock, a sight of the sun put us a few miles ahead of our dead-reckoning position. We were quite close now. At 1.14 o'clock, Greenwich civil time, our calculations showed that we were at the Pole. I opened the trapdoor and dropped over the calculated position of the Pole the small flag which was weighted with the stone from **Bennett's grave**. Stone and flag plunged down together. The flag had been advanced 1,500 miles further south than it had ever been advanced by any American expedition.

For a few seconds we stood over the spot there Amundsen had stood, 14 December 1911; and where Scott had also stood, thirty-four days later, reading the note which Amundsen had left for him. In their honour, the flags of their countries were again carried over the Pole. There was nothing now to mark that scene: only a white desolation and solitude disturbed by the sound of our engines. The Pole lay in the centre of a limitless plain. To the right, which is to say to the eastward, the horizon was covered with clouds. If mountains lay there, as some geologists believe, they were concealed and we had no hint of them.

And that, in brief, is all there is to tell about the South Pole. One gets there, and that is about all there is for the telling. It is the effort to get there that counts.

We put the Pole behind us and raced for home.

Bennett's grave: Floyd Bennett had flown the plane that took Richard Byrd on the first flight over the North Pole in 1926.

Bush etiquette and bear traps

from Travels in West Africa

by Mary Kingsley OBE (1862–1900)

Mary Kingsley was a rare species. She was a female travel writer in Victorian times. She had a great sense of fun, and was always ready to laugh at herself. In this extract she meets the Fan tribe and learns some harsh lessons about polite behaviour in the West African bush, and what to do if you fall into a trap.

A certain sort of friendship soon arose between the **Fan** and me. We each recognised that we belonged to that same section of the human race with whom it is better to drink than to fight. We knew we would each have killed the other, if sufficient inducement were offered, and so we took a certain amount of care that the inducement should not arise. Grey Shirt and Pagan also, their trade friends, the Fans treated with an independent sort of courtesy; but Silence, Singlet, the Passenger, and above all Ngouta, they openly did not care a row of pins for, and I have small doubt that had it not been for us other three they would have killed and eaten these very amiable gentlemen with as much compunction as an English sportsman would kill as many rabbits. They on their part hated the Fan, and never lost an opportunity of telling me 'these Fan be bad man too much'.

I must not forget to mention the other member of our party, a Fan gentleman with the manners of a duke and the habits of a dustbin. He came with us, quite uninvited

---

Fan: Members of the tribe now known as the 'Fang'

by me, and never asked for any pay; I think he only wanted to see the fun, and drop in for a fight if there was one going on, and to pick up the pieces generally. He was evidently a man of some importance, from the way the others treated him; and moreover he had a splendid gun, with a gorilla-skin sheath for its lock, and ornamented all over its stock with brass nails. His costume consisted of a small piece of dirty rag round his loins; and whenever we were going through dense undergrowth, or wading a swamp, he wore that filament tucked up scandalously short. Whenever we were sitting down in the forest having one of our nondescript meals, he always sat next to me and appropriated the tin. Then he would fill his pipe and, turning to me with the easy grace of aristocracy, would say what may be translated as 'My dear Princess, could you favour me with a **lucifer**?'

I used to say, 'My dear Duke, charmed, I'm sure', and give him one ready-lit.

I dared not trust him with the box whole, having a personal conviction that he would have kept it. I asked him what he would do suppose I was not there with the box of lucifers; and he produced a bush-cow's horn with a neat wood lid tied on with tie tie, and from out of it he produced a flint and steel and demonstrated. Unfortunately, all his Grace's minor possessions, owing to the scantiness of his attire, were in one and the same pineapple-fibre bag which he wore slung across his shoulder; and these possessions, though not great, were as dangerous to the body as a million sterling is said to be to the soul, for they consisted largely of gunpowder and snuff, and their separate receptacles leaked and their contents commingled, so that demonstration on fire-making methods among the Fan ended in an awful bang and blow-up in a small way, and the Professor and his

---

lucifer: a phosphorous match

pupil sneezed like fury for ten minutes, and a cruel world laughed till it nearly died, for twenty. Still, that bag with all its failings was a wonder for its containing power.

Kiva, who was the only one among us who had been to Efoua, said that unless we [hurried] we should not reach Efoua that night. I said, 'Why not stay for bush?', not having contracted any love for a night in a Fan town by the experience of M'fetta; moreover, the Fans were not sure that after all the whole party of us might not spend the evening at Efoua, when we did get there, simmering in its cooking-pots . . .

About five o'clock I was off ahead and noticed a path which I had been told I should meet with, and, when met with, I must follow. The path was slightly indistinct, but by keeping my eye on it I could see it. Presently I came to a place where it went out, but appeared again on the other side of a clump of underbush fairly distinctly. I made a short cut for it and the next news was I was in a heap, on a lot of spikes, some fifteen feet or so below ground level, at the bottom of a bag-shaped game pit.

It is at these times you realise the blessing of a good thick skirt. Had I paid heed to the advice of many people in England, who ought to have known better, and did not do it themselves, and adopted masculine garments, I should have been spiked to the bone, and done for. Whereas, save for a good many bruises, here I was with the fulness of my skirt tucked under me, sitting on nine ebony spikes some twelve inches long, in comparative comfort, howling lustily to be hauled out. The duke came along first, and looked down at me. I said, 'Get a bush-rope, and haul me out.' He grunted and sat down on a log. The Passenger came next, and he looked down. 'You kill?' says he. 'Not much,' say I; 'Get a bush-rope and haul me out.' '**No fit**,' says he, and sat down on the log.

'**No fit**': 'Not a chance!'

Presently, however, Kiva and Wiki came up, and Wiki went and selected the one and only bush-rope suitable to haul an English lady, of my exact complexion, age, and size, out of that one particular pit. They seemed rare round there from the time he took; and I was just casting about in my mind as to what method would be best to employ in getting up the smooth, yellow, sandy-clay, in-curved walls, when he arrived with it, and I was out in a twinkling, and very much ashamed of myself, until Silence, who was then leading, disappeared through the path before us with a despairing yell. Each man then pulled the skin cover off his gun lock, carefully looked to see if things there were all right and ready loosened his knife in its snake-skin sheath; and then we set about hauling poor Silence out, binding him up where necessary with cool green leaves; for he, not having a skirt, had got a good deal frayed at the edges on those spikes.

A perilous ascent

from A Lady's Life in the Rocky Mountains
by Isabella Bird

Isabella Bird was a clergyman's daughter from Cheshire. In 1854 she was sent to America and Canada by her doctor to 'improve her health'. In 1873 she set off on an expedition to the Rocky Mountains.

This extract describes her ascent of Long's Peak. The mountain was 14,700 feet (4,480 metres) high and had been climbed for the first time only five years before.

At **the 'Notch'** the real business of the ascent began. Two thousand feet of solid rock towered above us, four thousand feet of broken rock shelved precipitously below; smooth granite ribs, with barely a foothold, stood out here and there; melted snow, refrozen several times, presented a more serious obstacle; many of the rocks were loose, and tumbled down when touched. To me it was a time of extreme terror. I was roped to '**Jim**', but it was of no use, my feet were paralysed and slipped on the bare rock, and he said it was useless to try to go that way, and we retraced our steps. I wanted to return to the 'Notch', knowing that my incompetence would detain the party, and one of the young men said almost plainly that a woman was a dangerous encumbrance, but the trapper replied shortly that if it were not to take a lady up he would not go up at all. He went on to explore, and reported that further progress on the correct line of ascent was blocked by ice; and then for two hours we descended, lowering ourselves

---

the 'Notch': a feature of the mountain – a high pass
'**Jim**': 'Mountain Jim', a local trapper and guide

by our hands from rock to rock along a boulder-strewn sweep of 4000 feet patched with ice and snow, and perilous from rolling stones. My fatigue, giddiness, and pain from bruised ankles, and arms half pulled out of their sockets, were so great that I should never have gone half-way had not 'Jim', **nolens volens**, dragged me along with a patience and skill, and withal a determination that I should ascend the Peak, which never failed. After descending about 2000 feet to avoid the ice, we got into a deep ravine with inaccessible sides, partly filled with ice and snow and partly with large and small fragments of rock, which were constantly giving way, rendering the footing very insecure. That part to me was two hours of painful and unwilling submission to the inevitable; of trembling, slipping, straining, of smooth ice appearing when it was least expected, and of weak entreaties to be left behind while the others went on. 'Jim' always said that there was no danger, that there was only a short bad bit ahead, and that I should go up even if he carried me!

Slipping, faltering, gasping from the exhausting toil in the rarefied air, with throbbing hearts and panting lungs, we reached the top of the gorge and squeezed ourselves between two gigantic fragments of rock by a passage called the 'Dog's Lift', when I climbed on the shoulders of one man and then was hauled up. This introduced us by an abrupt turn round the south-west angle of the Peak to a narrow shelf of considerable length, rugged, uneven, and so overhung by the cliff in some places that it is necessary to crouch to pass at all. Above, the peak looks nearly vertical for 400 feet; and below, the most tremendous precipice I have ever seen descends in one unbroken fall. This is usually considered the most dangerous part of the ascent, but it does not seem so to me, for such foothold as there is is secure, and one

---

nolens volens: [Latin] whether I wanted to or not

fancies that it is possible to hold on with the hands. But there, and on the final, and, to my thinking, the worst part of the climb, one slip, and a breathing, thinking, human being would lie 3000 feet below, a shapeless, bloody heap! '**Ring**' refused to traverse the Ledge, and remained at the 'Lift' howling piteously.

As we crept from the lodge round a horn of rock, I beheld what made me perfectly sick and dizzy to look at – the terminal Peak itself – a smooth, cracked face or wall of pink granite, as nearly perpendicular as anything could well be up which it was possible to climb, well deserving the name of the 'American Matterhorn'.

Scaling, not climbing, is the correct term for this last ascent. It took one hour to accomplish 500 feet, pausing for breath every minute or two. The only foothold was in narrow cracks or on minute projections on the granite. To get a toe in these cracks, or here and there on a scarcely obvious projection, while crawling on hands and knees, all the while tortured with thirst and gasping and struggling for breath, this was the climb; but at last the Peak was won. A grand, well-defined mountain-top it is, a nearly level acre of boulders, with precipitous sides all round, the one we came up being the only accessible one.

It was not possible to remain long. One of the young men was seriously alarmed by bleeding from the lungs, and the intense dryness of the day and the rarefaction of the air, at a height of nearly 15,000 feet, made **respiration** very painful. These is always water on the Peak, but it was frozen as hard as a rock, and the sucking of ice and snow increases thirst. We all suffered severely from the want of water, and the gasping for breath made our mouths and tongues so dry that articulation was difficult, and the speech of all unnatural.

---

respiration: breathing
Ring: Jim's dog

From the summit were seen in unrivalled combination all the views which had rejoiced our eyes during the ascent. It was something at last to stand upon the storm-rent crown of this lonely sentinel of the Rocky Range, on one of the mightiest of the vertebrae of the backbone of the North American continent, and to see the waters start from both oceans. Uplifted above love and hate and storms of passion, calm amidst the eternal silences, fanned by **zephyrs** and bathed in living blue, peace rested for that once bright day on the Peak, as if it were some region

'Where falls not rain, or hail, or any snow,
Or ever wind blows loudly.'

We placed our names, with the date of ascent, in a tin within a crevice and descended to the Ledge, sitting on the smooth granite, getting our feet into cracks and against projections, and letting ourselves down by our hands, 'Jim' going before me, so that I might steady my feet against his powerful shoulders. I was no longer giddy, and faced the precipice of 3500 feet without a shiver. Repassing the Ledge and Lift, we accomplished the descent through 1500 feet of ice and snow, with many falls and bruises, but no worse mishap, and there separated, the young men taking the steepest but most direct way to the Notch, with the intention of getting ready for the march home, and 'Jim' and I taking what he thought the safer route for me – a descent over boulders for 2000 feet, and then a tremendous ascent to the 'Notch'. I had various falls, and once hung by my frock, which caught on a rock, and 'Jim' severed it with his hunting-knife, upon which I fell into a crevice full of soft snow. We were driven lower down the mountains than he had intended by impassable tracts of ice, and the ascent was tremendous. For the last 200 feet

---

zephyrs: gentle breezes

the boulders were of enormous size, and the steepness fearful. Sometimes I drew myself up on hands and knees, sometimes crawled; sometimes 'Jim' pulled me up by my arms or a **lariat**, and sometimes I stood on his shoulders, or he made steps for me of his feet and hands, but at six we stood on the Notch in the splendour of the sinking sun, all colour deepening, all peaks glorifying, all shadows purpling, all peril past.

---

lariat: lasso, a rope with a noose for catching wild animals

Driving hints and tips
from Holidays in Hell
by P.J. O'Rourke

P. J. O'Rourke shows that it's not necessary to explore uncharted wildernesses to experience a dangerous journey. Just going out on the roads in the developing world can provide its own share of thrills and spills! This extract takes a humorous look at some of the difficulties an American traveller can encounter behind the wheel.

Road hazards

What would be a road hazard anywhere else, in the Third World is probably the road. There are two techniques for coping with this. One is to drive very fast so your wheels 'get on top' of the ruts and your car sails over the ditches and gullies. Predictably, this will result in disaster. The other technique is to drive very slowly. This will also result in disaster. No matter how slowly you drive into a ten-foot hole, you're still going to get hurt. You'll find the locals themselves can't make up their minds. Either they drive at 2 m.p.h. – which they do every time there's absolutely no way to get around them. Or else, they drive at 100 m.p.h. – which they do coming right at you when you finally get a chance to pass the guy going 2 m.p.h..

Basic information

It's important to have your facts straight before you begin piloting a car around an underdeveloped country. For instance, which side of the road do they drive on? This is easy. They drive on your side. That is, you can depend on it, any oncoming traffic will be on your side of the road. Also, how do you translate kilometres into miles? Most people don't know this, but one kilometre = ten miles, exactly. True, a kilometre is only 62 per cent of a mile, but if something is one hundred kilometres away, read that as one thousand miles because the roads are 620 per cent worse than anything you've ever seen. And when you see a 50 k.p.h. speed limit, you might as well figure that means 500 m.p.h. because nobody cares.

Traffic signs and signals

Most developing nations use international traffic symbols. Americans may find themselves perplexed by road signs that look like Boy Scout merit badges and by such things as an iguana silhouette with a red diagonal bar across it. Don't worry, the locals don't know what they mean, either. The locals do, however, have an elaborate set of signals used to convey information to the traffic around

them. For example, if you're trying to pass someone and he blinks his left signal, it means go ahead. Either that or it means a large truck is coming around the bend, and you'll get killed if you try. You'll find out in a moment.

Signalling is further complicated by festive decorations found on many vehicles. It can be hard to tell a hazard flasher from a string of Christmas-tree lights wrapped around the bumper, and brake lights can be confused with the dozen red Jesus statuettes and the ten stuffed animals with blinking eyes on the package shelf.

Dangerous curves

Dangerous curves are marked, at least in Christian lands, by white wooden crosses positioned to make the curves even more dangerous. These crosses are memorials to people who've died in traffic accidents, and they give a rough statistical indication of how much trouble you're likely to have at that spot in the road. Thus, when you come through a curve in a full-power slide and are suddenly confronted with a veritable forest of crucifixes, you know you're dead.

Learning to drive like a local

It's important to understand that in the Third World most driving is done with the horn, or 'Egyptian Brake Pedal', as it is known. There is a precise and complicated etiquette of horn use. Honk your horn only under the following circumstances:

1 When anything blocks the road.
2 When anything doesn't.
3 When anything might.
4 At red lights.
5 At green lights.
6 All other times.

A slight hitch in Luxembourg
from Neither Here nor There
by Bill Bryson

Bad driving can be found anywhere. Bill Bryson finds that drivers in Luxembourg aren't going to win any road-safety prizes either.

The driver was very friendly. He spoke good English and shouted at me over the lawnmower roar of the engine that he worked as a travelling shoe salesman and his wife was a clerk in a Luxembourg bank and that they lived just over the border in Arlon. He kept turning round to rearrange things on the back seat to give me more space, throwing shoeboxes at the back windowsill, which I would have preferred him not to do because more often than not they clonked me on the head, and at the same time he was driving with one hand at seventy miles an hour in heavy traffic.

Every few seconds his wife would shriek as the back of a lorry loomed up and filled the windscreen, and he would attend to the road for perhaps two and a half seconds before returning his attention to my comfort. She constantly berated him for his driving but he acted as if this were some engaging quirk of hers, and kept throwing me mugging, conspiratorial, deeply Gallic looks, as if her squeaky bitching were a private joke between the two of us.

I have seldom been more certain that I was about to die. The man drove as if we were in an arcade game. The highway was a three-lane affair – something else I had never seen before – with one lane going east, one lane going west and a shared middle lane for overtaking from either direction. My new friend did not appear to grasp the system. He would zip into the middle lane and seem genuinely astonished to find a forty-ton truck bearing down on us like something out of a Road Runner cartoon. He would veer out of the way at the last possible instant and then hang out of the window shouting abuse at the passing driver, before being shrieked back to the next crisis by me and his wife. I later learned that Luxembourg has the highest highway fatality rate in Europe, which does not surprise me in the smallest degree.

How to hang on to your backpack
from Pickpockets and Thieves
artoftravel.com

Travelling can still be a dangerous activity. This extract is taken from a popular backpackers' website.

Pickpockets and Thieves

Address: http://www.

Most visitors to European and other countries don't encounter pickpockets to thieves, regardless of how or where valuables are carried. In one developing North African country with a rap for rip-offs only five per cent of visitors are a victim of thievery, according to a survey in a British magazine. In your travels you will mostly experience waitresses chasing you down with a forgotten camera, taxi drivers taking the best route, other backpackers looking out for your stuff, the correct change in your hand time after time, the shining honesty and kindness of most people.

Nevertheless, the trouble and expense of replacing passports, tickets, travellers cheques, and gear can wreak havoc on your tour.

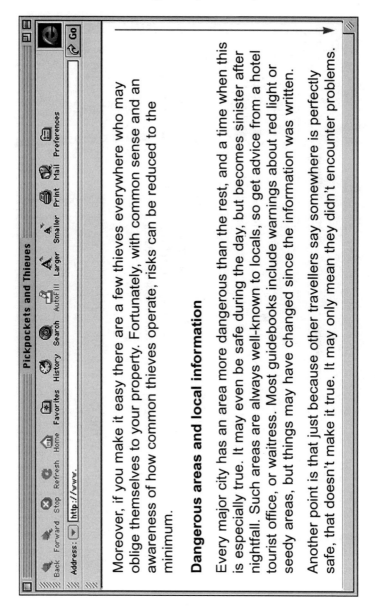

Moreover, if you make it easy there are a few thieves everywhere who may oblige themselves to your property. Fortunately, with common sense and an awareness of how common thieves operate, risks can be reduced to the minimum.

Dangerous areas and local information

Every major city has an area more dangerous than the rest, and a time when this is especially true. It may even be safe during the day, but becomes sinister after nightfall. Such areas are always well-known to locals, so get advice from a hotel tourist office, or waitress. Most guidebooks include warnings about red light or seedy areas, but things may have changed since the information was written.

Another point is that just because other travellers say somewhere is perfectly safe, that doesn't make it true. It may only mean they didn't encounter problems.

Back Forward Stop Refresh Home Favorites History Search AutoFill Larger Smaller Print Mail Preferences

Address: http://www.

I listened to an experienced backpacker swear how the dangers of a particular area were highly exaggerated or non-existent, when the previous day I had spoken to three Germans who had been robbed at gunpoint there.

Local authorities and tourist offices cannot always be relied upon, either, as they may have an interest in minimising problems, so you always need to use your eyes, ears, brain, instincts and best judgement, along with at least a few degrees of body lean towards safety, away from recklessness.

Pickpockets

As you wait in line at the crowded Amsterdam tourist office, continuously blaring over the loudspeaker is this warning in six languages: 'Your attention, please. Watch your wallets, there are pickpockets about!'

Pickpockets and Thieves

Address: http://www.

That tourist office is tough pickings for any would-be pickpockets, as everyone is continuously fidgeting with pockets or purses, and throwing about a great many suspicious looks.

The professional pickpocket in the developed world has a more-or-less standard operating procedure. He chooses a likely target – someone who obviously has money within easy reach, which includes back pockets and purses. If the thief cannot get the money cleanly, he or a partner will create a distraction by bumping the target, violently colliding with the target, or spilling something on the target. The wallet is snatched and within two seconds discreetly handed to a partner who quickly walks away. The money and valuables are removed and the rest dumped with in a few more seconds.

Even if you see or feel what is happening, you have no evidence. The scoundrel

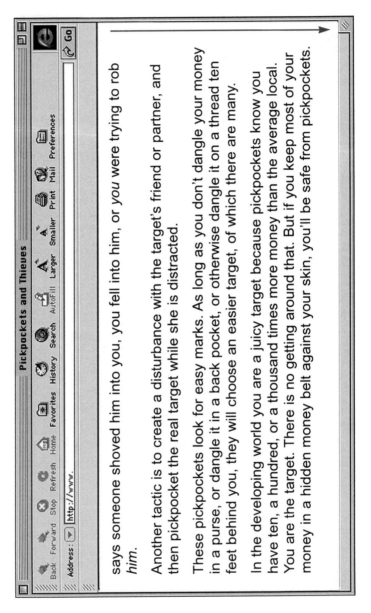

says someone shoved him into you, you fell into him, or *you* were trying to rob *him*.

Another tactic is to create a disturbance with the target's friend or partner, and then pickpocket the real target while she is distracted.

These pickpockets look for easy marks. As long as you don't dangle your money in a purse, or dangle it in a back pocket, or otherwise dangle it on a thread ten feet behind you, they will choose an easier target, of which there are many.

In the developing world you are a juicy target because pickpockets know you have ten, a hundred, or a thousand times more money than the average local. You are the target. There is no getting around that. But if you keep most of your money in a hidden money belt against your skin, you'll be safe from pickpockets.

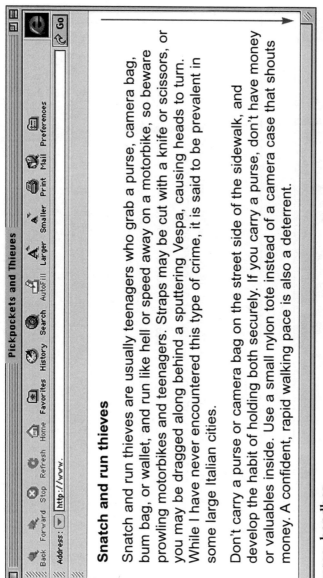

Pickpockets and Thieves

Address: http://www.

Snatch and run thieves

Snatch and run thieves are usually teenagers who grab a purse, camera bag, bum bag, or wallet, and run like hell or speed away on a motorbike, so beware prowling motorbikes and teenagers. Straps may be cut with a knife or scissors, or you may be dragged along behind a sputtering Vespa, causing heads to turn. While I have never encountered this type of crime, it is said to be prevalent in some large Italian cities.

Don't carry a purse or camera bag on the street side of the sidewalk, and develop the habit of holding both securely. If you carry a purse, don't have money or valuables inside. Use a small nylon tote instead of a camera case that shouts money. A confident, rapid walking pace is also a deterrent.

purse: handbag
sidewalk: pavement

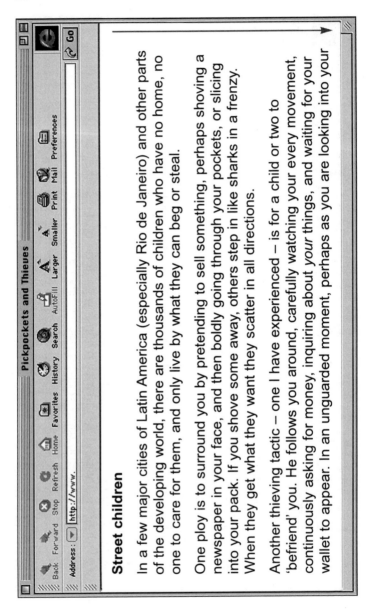

Pickpockets and Thieves

Address: http://www.

Street children

In a few major cities of Latin America (especially Rio de Janeiro) and other parts of the developing world, there are thousands of children who have no home, no one to care for them, and only live by what they can beg or steal.

One ploy is to surround you by pretending to sell something, perhaps shoving a newspaper in your face, and then boldly going through your pockets, or slicing into your pack. If you shove some away, others step in like sharks in a frenzy. When they get what they want they scatter in all directions.

Another thieving tactic – one I have experienced – is for a child or two to 'befriend' you. He follows you around, carefully watching your every movement, continuously asking for money, inquiring about *your* things, and waiting for your wallet to appear. In an unguarded moment, perhaps as you are looking into your

Pickpockets and Thieves

Back Forward Stop Refresh Home Favorites History Search AutoFill Larger Smaller Print Mail Preferences

Address: http://www.

wallet to give him a few cruzados, or to make another transaction with someone else, he grabs whatever he can and runs.

Of course these children have been dealt an awful hand in life, and are just trying to survive. And while you probably want to be compassionate, I suggest giving to local aid agencies, if possible. It is simply too risky to embolden the hungry and desperate with ultimately insignificant gifts of sweets or money.

The best defence, as always, is to maintain a low profile and travel lightly. A hidden money belt is a necessity. In high-crime and street-urchin areas do not encourage even one child, as others may follow. Locals often treat street children like dogs, completely ignoring or threatening them. While I don't think many travellers can do that, you must keep your own safety in mind.

Activities

An unexpected ducking

1 Have you ever been on, or wanted to go on an adventure holiday or work abroad with an organisation like VSO (Voluntary Service Overseas)? What part of the world would you want to visit? Why?

2 Write a short local newspaper report of the accident. Remember to answer the questions: *What* happened? *Who* was involved? *Where* did it happen? *Why* and *how* did it happen? Include:

   - a **snappy heading** to attract readers
   - a **new paragraph for each topic** below:
     - what it was like when they set out
     - when they realised they were in danger
     - what happened to the people
     - the rescue
     - returning to the rest of their group.

   Include one or two quotes, and say how Pam felt at the end. Describe the picture you would show.

3 How does the writer use **adjectives** (words that describe nouns, e.g. *muddy* torrent) to help build up an impression of what happened? In pairs, copy out and complete a chart like the one below to help you.

River	People/belongings
muddy torrent	*unstable* peki-peki
huge logs	*frail* craft
Surroundings	**Back in safety**
emerald forest	*dripping* wet
magnificent sunset	*hot* kebabs

4 Now look at question 1 on on page 37.

The flight over the South Pole (1929)

1 At the end of the extract the writer says: 'One gets there, and that is about all there is for the telling. It is the effort to get there that counts.' What effort did the flight take, and how does the writer help the reader understand it? Think about how he describes:

- the situation they were in (paragraph 1)
- the decisions they had to make (paragraphs 2–6)
- what happened and how they felt when they reached the South Pole (paragraph 7–end).

2 Richard Byrd had to decide very quickly whether to lose weight by dumping food or fuel. What might have been his argument for and against each option? In groups, make a list of advantages and disadvantages for dumping either food or fuel.

3 The situation the writer describes is tense, immediate and full of action. Copy out two tables which start like the ones below. In pairs:

a choose good examples of **verbs** the writer has used.
b explain how each verb is used to help make the action vivid.

Verbs used of the plane	
creeping	Shows that the aeroplane seemed to be moving very slowly and hesitantly
bob	
slide	
Verbs used of the people	
signalled	Shows that the sign Byrd made was an order
yell	
gesticulate	

4 Now look at question 1 on page 37.

Bush etiquette and bear traps

1 The writer gives the reader a lot of detail about the people she meets and travels with. Make brief notes on what the reader learns about:

  a the Fan
  b Grey Shirt and Pagan
  c Silence, Singlet, the Passenger and Nguouta
  d a Fan 'gentleman'.

2 It was unusual for women to travel in Victorian times. Make brief notes about what the reader learns about Mary Kingsley. Include:

  • her sense of adventure and courage
  • her sense of humour
  • how she dressed.

3 The writing includes some quotes in dialect. Write out the following phrases in modern English.

  'these Fan be bad men too much' (page 8, paragraph 1)
  'could you favour me with a lucifer?' (page 9, paragraph 1)
  'Why not stay for bush?' (page 10, paragraph 2)
  'the next news was . . .' (page 10, paragraph 3)

4 Now look at question 1 on page 37.

A perilous ascent

1 Isabella Bird wrote this account over a hundred years ago, so some words may be unfamiliar, or their meaning may have changed. In pairs, use a dictionary or a thesaurus. Write down modern English equivalents of the words and phrases below.

precipitously (page 12)
fatigue (page 13)
entreaties (page 13)
beheld (page 14)
the want of water (page 14)
rejoiced our eyes (page 15)
severed (page 15)

encumbrance (page 12)
rendering (page 13)
rarefied (page 13)
minute (page 14)
articulation (page 14)
mishap (page 15)

2 The ascent and descent are described in great detail through 6 stages. Make notes about the terrain, what happened to Isabella and the climbers' thoughts at each stage:

- stage 1 – climbing from the 'Notch'
- stage 2 – descending for 2 hours
- stage 3 – coming out of the gorge
- stage 4 – the ascent
- stage 5 – at the summit
- stage 6 – descending from the summit.

3 Imagine that you are one of the young men accompanying Isabella Bird on her climb. Write a letter to a friend describing the climb and Isabella's part in it. Say whether you admire her courage or feel that the expedition was slowed down or even endangered by her presence, and justify your opinions. Share the letters with the rest of the group. What is the balance of opinion? Is there a difference between what most girls and most boys think?

4 Now look at question 1 on page 37.

Driving Hints and Tips and A Slight Hitch in Luxembourg

1 These extracts are examples of travel journalism that is witty and humorous in style. They take a personal approach, making observations in a way that is intended to entertain, often using:

- exaggeration (e.g. *they drive at 2mph or at 100 mph*)
- generalisations (e.g. *you'll find the locals themselves can't make up their minds*)
- extreme statements (e.g. *Which side of the road do they drive on? This is easy. They drive on your side.*)

Find another good example of each of the above from **Driving Hints and Tips**. How do they make it clear that the writing is intended to entertain and not to cause offence or be taken seriously?

2 In **A Slight Hitch in Luxembourg**, how does Bill Bryson make his experience entertaining and vivid for the reader? Think about the way he describes the driver, the driver's wife and the traffic conditions and lets us 'in' on his own observations at the time.

3 The length of sentence used can help make humour more effective, for example:

Predictably, this will result in disaster. The other technique is to drive very slowly. This will also result in disaster. (P.J. O'Rourke)

Why is the effect of these short sentences humorous? Find a sentence in the Bill Bryson extract that uses a *long* sentence for the same purpose. Why do you think the writers chose short or long sentences? Can you find other examples of short or long sentences that the writers use to make their work humorous?

4 Write a short, funny account of real or imagined journey. Use exaggeration, generalisations and extreme statements. Vary your sentence length to help get the humour across.

5 Now look at question 1 on page 37.

How to hang on to your backpack

1 What does this extract tell you about:

- the sort of people you may meet on your travels
- what can cause lots of trouble and expense
- what advice to get when travelling in any city
- what can happen if you listen only to other travellers' advice
- where and how pickpockets are likely to operate
- how not to be the target of snatch and run thieves
- the best way to give to local street children?

2 Emails are often written in informal English. Write out the following slang phrases in formal English:

a . . . with a rap for rip-offs . . . (page 22)
b . . . who may oblige themselves to your property. (page 23)
c . . . along with at least a few degrees of body lean towards safety . . . (page 24)
d . . . easy marks . . . (page 26)
e . . . that shouts money . . . (page 27)

3 Design your own web page to alert visitors to any dangers in your area or an area you have visited.

- Use some headings to structure your material, such as: when arriving; when out walking; when out at night; what to do if asked for money
- You could divide your material into **Do's** and **Don't's** (e.g. **Do** keep your money in a safe place; **Don't** keep lots of money on your person).

4 Now look at question 1 on page 37.

Comparing texts

1 Each piece of travel writing has a particular purpose. The **language** and **structure** of a piece of writing helps get this purpose across to the reader. For each extract in this section use a format like the one on page 194 (see a completed example on page 196) to write a report on how these pieces of travel writing achieve their effect.

2 In groups, imagine you have been given unlimited funds to go on a dangerous journey of your choice. Where would you go? What would you do? Who would you take?

3 Which extract did you most and least enjoy in this section? Look back at the reports you have completed on the **text type**, **language**, **tone**, **narrator**, **address** and **period** of the extracts, to help explain your choice.

4 Choose one of the extracts below and rewrite it in the style suggested. Make sure you use the features that you have identified as belonging to that style.

Extract	Rewrite in the style of
Bush etiquette and bear traps (pages 8–11) From page 10 para 3 'About 5 o'clock . . .' to page 11'. . .frayed at the edges on those spikes'.	→ **How to hang on to your backpack** (pages 22–29) Internet advice for female travellers in the African bush
A perilous ascent (pages 12–16) From page 12 para 1 'At the Notch . . .' to end page 14 para 1 '. . . howling piteously'.	→ **Driving Hints and Tips** (pages 17–19) Ironic advice on the dangers and discomforts of mountaineering

5 Choose one of the styles in this section to write about a dangerous journey that you have experienced, or that you

have read about or researched. Remember to include the features that you have studied for that style, and to:

- **make your descriptions vivid** – you could include adjectives that help give the feeling of danger, for example 'a *despairing* yell' (Mary Kingsley), 'a *shapeless, bloody* heap' (Isabella Bird).
- **make the action and what happened clear** – you could include verbs that show the kind of experience taking place: for example, 'whirlpools *tugging* at the hull' (John Blashford-Snell), 'he would *zip* into the middle lane' (Bill Bryson)
- **make your writing interesting** by varying your sentence lengths for effect – short sentences for quick, terse statements such as 'Never look where you're going – you'll only scare yourself' (P. J. O'Rourke) and longer sentences to give the effect of greater reflection – for example, the opening sentence of Richard Byrd's account of his flight to the South Pole (page 5).

You should **structure your work** with an arresting opening, interesting development and exciting or unusual ending, using:

- headings
- paragraphs
- a variety of complete sentences.

The Great Outdoors

For most people, travel is about holidays: a time for rest and relaxation somewhere with a warm climate, or interesting landscape, or lots of things to see and do. There's nothing like getting away from it all in the Great Outdoors…

An American student arrives in the UK

from Notes from a Small Island
by Bill Bryson

Of course, to most of the world, England is a foreign country. Bill Bryson is one of the funniest writers around, especially when he is writing about his attempts, as an American, to understand the English. It all started when he arrived in Dover for the first time, and found that it was shut …

Prologue

My first sight of England was on a foggy March night in 1973 when I arrived on the midnight ferry from Calais. For twenty minutes, the terminal area was aswarm with activity as cars and lorries poured forth, customs people did their duties, and everyone made for the London road.

Then abruptly all was silence and I wandered through sleeping, low-lit streets threaded with fog, just like in a **Bulldog Drummond** movie. It was rather wonderful having an English town all to myself.

The only mildly dismaying thing was that all the hotels and guesthouses appeared to be shut up for the night. I walked as far as the rail station, thinking I'd catch a train to London, but the station, too, was dark and shuttered. I was standing wondering what to do when I noticed a grey light of television filling an upstairs window of a guesthouse across the road. Hooray, I thought, someone awake, and hastened across, planning humble apologies to the kindly owner for the lateness of my arrival and imagining a cheery conversation which included the line, 'Oh, but I couldn't possibly ask you to feed me at this hour. No, honestly – well, if you're quite sure it's no trouble, then perhaps just a roast beef sandwich and a large dill pickle with perhaps some potato salad and a bottle of beer.' The front path was pitch dark and in my eagerness and unfamiliarity with British doorways, I tripped on a step, crashing face-first into the door and sending half a dozen empty milk bottles clattering. Almost immediately the upstairs window opened.

'Who's that?' came a sharp voice.

I stepped back, rubbing my nose, and peered up at a silhouette with hair curlers. 'Hello, I'm looking for a room,' I said.

'We're shut.'

'Oh.' But what about my supper?

'Try the Churchill. On the front.'

'On the front of what?' I asked, but the window was already banging closed.

Bulldog Drummond: a forerunner of James Bond in British black-and-white movies of the 1940s and 1950s

The Churchill was sumptuous and well lit and appeared ready to receive visitors. Through a window I could see people in suits in a bar, looking elegant and suave, like characters from a **Noel Coward** play. I hesitated in the shadows, feeling like a street urchin. I was **socially and sartorially ill-suited** for such an establishment and anyway it was clearly beyond my meagre budget. Only the previous day, I had handed over an exceptionally plump wad of colourful francs to a beady-eyed **Picardy** hotelier in payment for one night in a lumpy bed and a plate of mysterious *chasseur* containing the bones of assorted small animals, much of which had to be secreted away in a large napkin in order not to appear impolite, and had determined thenceforth to be more cautious with expenditures. So I turned reluctantly from the Churchill's beckoning warmth and trudged off into the darkness.

Further along Marine Parade stood a shelter, open to the elements but roofed, and I decided that this was as good as I was going to get. With my backpack for a pillow, I lay down and drew my jacket tight around me. The bench was slatted and hard and studded with big roundheaded bolts that made reclining in comfort an impossibility – doubtless their intention. I lay for a long time listening to the sea washing over the shingle below, and eventually dropped off to a long, cold night of mumbled dreams in which I found myself being pursued over Arctic ice floes by a beady-eyed Frenchman with a catapult, a bag of bolts, and an uncanny aim, who thwacked me repeatedly in the buttocks and legs for

---

Noel Coward: British actor, singer and playwright noted for being terribly clever and witty while wearing a dinner jacket
socially and sartorially ill-suited: too unsophisticated and badly-dressed
Picardy: a region of Northern France
chausseur: stew

stealing a linen napkin full of seepy food and leaving it at the back of a dresser drawer of my hotel room. I awoke with a gasp about three, stiff all over and quivering from cold. The fog had gone. The air was now still and clear, and the sky was bright with stars. A beacon from the lighthouse at the far end of the breakwater swept endlessly over the sea. It was all most fetching, but I was far too cold to appreciate it. I dug shiveringly through my backpack and extracted every potentially warming item I could find – a flannel shirt, two sweaters, an extra pair of jeans. I used some woollen socks as mittens and put a pair of flannel boxer shorts on my head as a kind of desperate headwarmer, then sank heavily back onto the bench and waited patiently for death's sweet kiss. Instead, I fell asleep.

I was awakened again by an abrupt bellow of foghorn, which nearly knocked me from my narrow perch, and sat up feeling wretched but fractionally less cold. The world was bathed in that milky pre-dawn light that seems to come from nowhere. Gulls wheeled and cried over the water. Beyond them, past the stone breakwater, a ferry, vast and well lit, slid regally out to sea. I sat there for some time, a young man with more on his mind than in it. Another booming moan from the ship's foghorn passed over the water, re-exciting the **irksome** gulls. I took off my sock mittens and looked at my watch. It was 5.55 a.m. I looked at the receding ferry and wondered where anybody would be going at that hour. Where would *I* go at that hour? I picked up my back pack and shuffled off down the prom, to get some circulation going.

Near the Churchill, now itself peacefully sleeping, I came across an old guy walking a little dog. The dog was frantically trying to pee on every vertical surface and in

---

irksome: irritating, tiresome

consequence wasn't so much walking as being dragged along on three legs.

The man nodded a good-morning as I drew level. 'Might turn out nice,' he announced, gazing hopefully at a sky that looked like a pile of wet towels. I asked him if there was a restaurant anywhere that might be open. He knew of a place not far away and directed me to it. 'Best transport caff in Kent,' he said.

'Transport calf?' I repeated uncertainly, and retreated a couple of paces as I'd noticed his dog was straining desperately to moisten my leg.

'Very popular with the lorry drivers. They always know the best places, don't they?' He smiled amiably then lowered his voice a fraction and leaned towards me as if about to share a confidence. 'You might want to take them pants off your head before you go in.'

I clutched my head – 'Oh!' – and removed the forgotten boxer shorts with a blush. I tried to think of a **succinct** explanation, but the man was scanning the sky again.

'Definitely brightening up,' he decided, and dragged his dog off in search of new uprights. I watched them go, then turned and walked off down the promenade as it began to spit with rain.

---

succinct: expressed in a clear and brief way

Travels in Egypt

from Around the World in Eighty Days
by Michael Palin

Jules Verne was a nineteenth-century writer of exciting science fiction and fantasy stories such as *Around the World in Eighty Days*, *20,000 Leagues Under the Sea* and *Journey to the Centre of the Earth*.

In 1988, Michael Palin decided to see if he could bring fiction to life. Accompanied by a BBC film crew, he attempted to travel around the world in only eighty days. 'Easy!' you might say, 'get on a plane!' However, Palin was only allowed to use 'old-fashioned' travel methods, which meant no planes.

In this extract, Palin has been travelling for only seven days. He arrives in Egypt. All is going well – so far . . .

DAY 7
1 OCTOBER

Once on Egyptian soil, I feel a curious surge of adrenaline, as if I've escaped from five days in cotton wool. There'll be no such thing as normal for quite a while now. As if to underline this I find myself in a fiacre, which is an open horse-drawn cab, being galloped out of the port and into the hurtling traffic. A gaggle of Egyptians, sipping tea, have presumably been told what the camera's there for.

'You are Michael Caine?' they shout.

'No. I am cheaper than Michael Caine.'

They all laugh, beyond the limits of politeness. 'We want to see this film very quickly.'

I just want to survive long enough to make it, but there's not time to tell this as Achmed the driver applies his whip and we swing out into the streets of Alexandria. It's quite terrifying. The horse, which for some reason is called Larry, seems **congenitally** unable to move in a straight line and in a series of lurches and wild whip-assisted sprints, dodging within inches of passing cars, we eventually reach the famous Corniche – the long curving sea-front. It's like Cannes with acne. A wide and well-proportioned road and some handsome **facades** in the **neoclassical** style, but everything blotchy and half patched-up, giving it the odd air of a city that was abandoned long ago and is now full of people gingerly coming back to re-inhabit.

On the sea-wall, **itinerant** street-sellers are curled up asleep, their heads protected from the sun inside the baskets they'll later sell. Achmed and Larry deliver me physically, if not mentally, unscathed to the Cecil Hotel. Here hippies are having their shoes shined by ten-year-olds and within the space of a minute I'm offered sunglasses, black market currency and a trip to **Alamein**.

'Alamein . . . you know . . . Hitler . . .'

Midday: To the impressive Misr Station to pick up a train to Cairo. The noise is incredible. This is a horn blower society. Egyptian drivers make New York cabbies sound like librarians. They must specially modify their cars to connect the accelerator to the horn. They never use one without the other. And now the **muezzin** has started, his **raucously** distorted call to prayer adding to the **cacophony**, and causing prayer mats to be laid down in the middle of an already packed ticket office.

---

congenitally: from birth **facades**: fronts of buildings
neo-classical: in the Ancient Greek or Roman style **itinerant**: wandering
Alamein: Egyptian village, scene of a decisive victory for the British 8th Army in World War II **muezzin**: in Islam, someone who calls Muslims to prayer **raucously**: harshly **cacophony**: loud noise

A blazing row has erupted as to whether we're allowed to film or not, and about four people are shouting at each other, clutching their heads. You'd think there'd been a death in the family the way they carry on. It all reminds me of a big, slightly out of control boys' public school, everyone issuing different orders, a few people trying to be serious, but everyone else finding it frightfully funny.

Watching the crowds come off the trains it's interesting to note how the traditional garb – **jellabas** and turbans and **fezzes** for men, and veils and long dresses for women – is now mixed with Western dress – Levis, jeans, slacks, shirts, dresses and skirts. The contrast is extraordinary – some look like Old Testament prophets, others like James Dean. Some times there's a mixture with the women, of the old Islamic headdress and a modern slightly blowsy **Orlon** two-piece. It may be chaotic but life wouldn't be as rich as this at airports, where people are much more conditioned, directed and cowed into submission.

Four o'clock: at Cairo station, half an hour late after a 220-kilometre train journey from Alex across the fertile, **feudally-farmed** Nile Delta. The temperature is 91 degrees.

It's Saturday afternoon and I've been promised seats for the big football match between local heroes National Sporting Club and some tough-tacklers from Middle Egypt – Al Minya. I arrive at Cairo Stadium, in a grandiose complex called Nasser City, halfway through the second half. The stadium is a wide, comfortable bowl with an electronic scoreboard and lush grass playing surface. The terraces are clean and well cared-for and put most British grounds to shame.

---

jellaba:long robe **fez**: a type of hat **Orlon**: artificial fabric, like nylon
feudally-farmed: small-scale cultivation with primitive equipment

I'm rather confused by the colours and enthusiastically cheer an Al Minya attack by mistake. I'm then taken in hand by some local supporters who explain who's who and offer me sunflower seeds. They are exceptionally friendly and, as Sporting Club score twice only moments after my arrival, clearly regard me as having **Bill Shankly**-like powers.

The 60,000 crowd is well-patrolled. Ten minutes before the end riot police with transparent shields, visors, helmets and long white sticks take up position around the touchline, facing the crowd like nervous **samurai**.

Outside, the army, consisting of thin and petrified teenagers, waits in trucks. But there seems to be no trouble. Indeed, some supporters produce prayer mats and fall to their knees as soon as they leave the ground.

On the way back from the match, traffic is so solid along a half-finished eight-lane super-highway that we are passed by an old woman in black on a donkey, leading a herd of goats up the side of the motorway. A red, rather unhealthily flushed sun descends slowly behind a hazy city skyline. Last night it was the crimson swallows; tonight, more menacingly, sunset brings the kites, flapping lazily around the eucalyptus trees.

Having arrived in Egypt six hundred years too late to see one of the Seven Wonders of the World – the Pharos lighthouse – I felt I couldn't leave without seeing one that still exists – the Pyramids. I had always presumed they were in the middle of nowhere, marooned in the desert. In fact they are within five minutes' walk of apartment blocks in the suburb of Giza. My first view of them is from a traffic jam on Pyramids Road. The 4600-year-old apex of the Great Pyramid pokes up from behind a block of flats. My first full-frontal view of the Pyramids provokes an

---

Bill Shankly: legendary manager of Liverpool Football Club
samurai: Japanese warriors who carried long swords

heretical comparison with the slag-heaps which used to litter the South Yorkshire countryside where I grew up. They had the same solid bulk, shape and immovable presence. Once free of the straggling suburb we are straightaway in desert. There's no transition through **savannah** and scrubland, like in the geography books. The city ends, the desert begins, and it goes on until you reach Morocco. The dustiness of Cairo is explained. Every time a wind blows it dumps thousands of tons of desert

 on the city. Closer now to the Pyramids and they are awesome. The blocks of sandstone at their base are twice as high as the small children playing around them. The structures rise serene and powerful above us, preserving an unmoving dignity, like great beasts surrounded by insects. Coaches ferry out an endless stream of human insects, deposit them at a tightly packed vantage point where they are assailed by camel-mongers, postcard salesmen, purveyors of trinkets and all the other free market forces which have ripped off tourists at this very spot for hundreds, if not thousands, of years.

They have their patter well worked out, and very bizarre it sounds in the middle of the desert:

'You from Yorkshire? . . . I am friend of Yorkshire!'

'You are English? Tally-ho!'

'What is your name?'

'Michael.'

'My camel's name is Michael!'

So it is that I find myself on a camel called Michael (or Ron or Julian or Nigel or Dwayne or Sheri-Anne) being

---

savannah: flat land with low vegetation

flung skywards into the air as the creature raises itself on its forelegs. It looks and feels grossly unsafe, as it totters into the desert with me clinging on for dear life and feeling ridiculously conspicuous in an Arab head-dress which the camel-owner, who I think is called Michael as well, has insisted I wear: 'Now you will be like Lawrence of Arabia!'

Behind me hot white people from all over the wealthy West are being given similar treatment. Every time they raise a camera to the Pyramids an Arab stands in front of it. The tourist adjusts his shot, the Arab follows. The air is full of the angry din of protest and dissension. This din is beginning to fade now as Michael, Michael and Michael wander further into the desert. In silence and sunset the Pyramids take on a potent, **talismanic** quality.

---

talismanic: with semi-magical, protective powers

Outdoor Excitement in Switzerland
from The Spirit of Adventure
Berner Oberland Magazine Summer 1999

The continuing reduction of the element of risk in everyday life seems to have encouraged a demand for 'extreme' experiences of one kind or another in a structured context – a demand which commercial organisations have been quick to fill. Would this extract from *Berner Oberland Magazine* persuade *you* to hurl yourself out of a helicopter from 4000 metres? Only you can tell ...

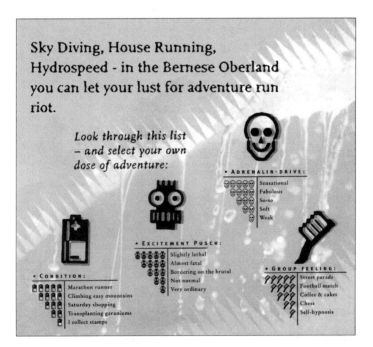

Sky Diving, House Running, Hydrospeed - in the Bernese Oberland you can let your lust for adventure run riot.

Look through this list – and select your own dose of adventure:

ADRENALIN-DRIVE:
Sensational
Fabulous
So-so
Soft
Weak

EXCITEMENT PUSCH:
Slightly lethal
Almost fatal
Bordering on the brutal
Not normal
Very ordinary

CONDITION:
Marathon runner
Climbing easy mountains
Saturday shopping
Transplanting geraniums
I collect stamps

GROUP FEELING:
Street parade
Football match
Coffee & cakes
Chess
Self-hypnosis

Eiger Jump

Perhaps you aren't quite as courageous as you first thought.

Or perhaps you hadn't realised what the Eiger Jump actually was. Unfortunately, it's too late now! 'He's got to be joking' is what you're probably thinking when the Jump Master tells you to part company with the helicopter at an altitude of around 4000 metres – that's about two and a half miles. After seemingly endless seconds you dare to open your eyes a little. You're free falling at 200 kilometres an hour – this is Sky Diving at its most spectacular. You see that towering trio of the Eiger, Mönch and Jungfrau, and you find yourself screaming. With joy. Finally comes that soft 'swoosh' of your parachute as you land safely on the ground. You did it! For the first time – but definitely not the last.

- *Eiger Jump:*
  Alpin Raft, Interlaken/Matten
  Tel. 033 823 41 00

- *Sky Diving:*
  Adventure World Interlaken
  Tel. 033 826 77 11

House Running

Tell your friends and family that you spent your holidays House Running – and you're sure to get some strange looks. You don't have to mention the nervous rumbling in your stomach. Just tell them about that fantastic feeling when you first stand at right angles to the wall, high above the ground. Let the rope pass through your hands. S-l-o-w-l-y at first, then with growing courage and confidence as the faces below you come nearer and nearer. Spiderman for a day – and you'll have a photo to prove it.

- *Alpin Raft, Interlaken / Matten,*
  Tel 033 823 41 00

- *Swiss Adventures, Boltigen*
  Tel. 033 773 73 73

Bungy Jumping

☠☠☠☠☠ 🔋

🙂🙂🙂🙂🙂🙂 ⚡

You look out of the cabin on the Schilthorn Aerial Cableway and a thousand thoughts flash through your mind. This is the world's highest Bungy Jump. And you've volunteered for it! Is it really 'only' 180 metres?

Will the rope really hold me? 'No problem', the instructors will tell you. But it's all right for them. Bungy jumping is their business. You take the plunge – at this stage of the game you've no option. Your scream (of delight?) echoes back from the Schilthorn. You've done it! And we're sure of one thing. The next time you're in an aerial cableway and it stops moving, you'll be the first to look for the bungy rope.

- *Adventure World Interlaken, Tel. 033 826 77 11*

- *Stockhorn Cable Railway:*
  Alpin Raft, Interlaken/Matten, Tel. 033 823 41 00

- *Canyon Jumping:*
  Grindelwald Mountaineering Centre
  Tel. 033 853 52 00

- *Gstaad Alpine Centre, Tel. 033 722 40 06*

Rock Climbing

'Which way do we go?' This question is a certainty
when the Climb Master stands at the foot of a rock
wall with his hesitant group of beginners. With
hiking there's usually a choice. With rock climbing,
there isn't – the only way is up. After a basic crash
course in climbing and safety techniques, you
quickly get the hang of it and confidently head for
the heights. This is excellent climbing country, and
when Sylvester Stallone was in training for
Cliffhanger he came to the Bernese Oberland. Where
else?

- *Addresses and telephone numbers in the Information
  Section*

River Rafting

☻☻☻☻   ▮▮▮
☻☻☻☻   𝄢𝄢𝄢𝄢

Even the fish shake their heads in disbelief when
they see some of the strange craft careering down
the rivers of the Bernese Oberland. Only a few
years ago River Rafting was the 'in' thing. These
days the talk is of Tubing, Hot Dog, Fun Yak and
hydrospeed. But whether solo or with a group,
whether you tackle the Simme, Saane or Lütschine,
you're up against the same unpredictable elements
and powerful forces of nature. Are you ready for the
challenge?

• *Check out all the offers in the Information Section*

Kerala and Trivandrum
from Lonely Planet Guide to South India

The Lonely Planet Guides are written for the traveller and backpacker, as well as for holidaymakers.

The following extract is about Kerala, a province on the south-west coast of India. With its beautiful scenery, hot sunshine and warm sea, Kerala is quickly becoming a popular destination for Western tourists.

Read on and decide whether you'd like to visit Kerala.

KERALA AT A GLANCE

Population: 33 million
Area: 38,864 sq km
Capital: Thiruvananthapuram
Main Language: Malayalam
Best time to go: October to March

Highlights
- Exploring the backwaters aboard a *kettuvallam* (rice-barge houseboat)
- an evening of Kathakali dance theatre
- Sun, surf and seafood on the beach at Kovalam or Varkala
- An early morning jungle walk at Periyar Wildlife Sanctuary

Locator & Map Index

Kozhikode (Calicut) p452
Thrissur p449
Munnar p427
Kochi (Cochin) p432
Alappuzha to Kollam p413
Fort Cochin p435
Ernakulam p438
Alappuzha (Alleppey) p415
Kottayam p419
Periyar Wildlife Sanctuary p423
Kollam (Quilon) p411
Varkala p408
Thiruvananthapuram (Trivandrum) p390
Kovalam Beach p399

Festivals
January – Great Elephant March, Thrissur, Alappuzha, Thiruvananthapuram
April /May – Pooram Festival, Thrissur
August/September – Onam, Statewide

Kerala

'The Great Outdoors'

Kerala, the land of green magic, is a narrow, fertile strip on the south-west coast of India, sandwiched between the Lakshadweep Sea and the Western ghats. The landscape is dominated by rice fields, mango and cashew-nut trees and, above all, coconut palms. The Western ghats, with their dense tropical forests, misty peaks, extensive ridges and ravines, have sheltered Kerala from mainland invaders and encouraged **maritime** contact with the outside world.

HISTORY

The early history of Kerala is documented in ancient Tamil scripts and Hindu mythology. According to legend Parasu Rama, an incarnation of **Vishnu**, threw his weapon from Kanayakumari across the sea. The sea subsequently receded to the point where the weapon landed, and the land of Kerala was born. Its fortunes waxed and waned as it competed with empires, kingdoms and small **fiefdoms** for territory and trade.

People have been sailing to Kerala in search of spices, sandalwood and ivory for at least 2000 years. In those days (late 15th century to the 16th century) Kerala was not only a spice centre in its own right,

maritime: by sea
Vishnu: Hindu god
fiefdoms: minor territories

but a transhipment point for spices from the **Moluccas**. And it was through Kerala that Chinese products and ideas found their way to the west. Even today, Chinese-style fishing nets are widely used.

Such contact with people from around the world has resulted in an intriguing blend of cultures and has given Malayalis (natives of Kerala) a **cosmopolitan** outlook, coupled with a tradition of seeking their fortunes elsewhere in India or overseas. You can generally find a Malayali in any nook or cranny of the world.

The present-day state of Kerala was created in 1956 and is one of the most progressive, literate and highly educated states in India. Another of Kerala's distinctions was that it had one of the first freely elected communist governments in the world (elected in 1957). Communists have been in and out of office in Kerala ever since.

The relatively **equitable** distribution of land and income, found rarely to the same degree elsewhere in India, is the direct result of successive communist governments in the state. Kerala's progressive social policies have had other benefits: infant mortality in Kerala is the lowest in India, and the literacy rate of around 90% is the highest in the country.

Perhaps more than anywhere else in India, getting around Kerala can be half the fun, particularly on the backwater trips along the coastal lagoons. Even

Moluccas: Indonesian islands lying between Borneo and New Guinea
cosmopolitan: sophisticated
equitable: fair

an agonisingly slow train can be a restful experience when you're in Kerala – watching the canals and palm trees cruising past the open windows of your carriage at 20km/h can bring on a state of near-spiritual **inertia**.

The state also has some of the best and most picturesque beaches in India. Best of all, Kerala has an easy-going, relaxed atmosphere unlike the bustle you find elsewhere in India.

Kerala's Religions

The population of Kerala is roughly 60% Hindu, 20% Muslim and 20% Christian.

Kerala's main Christian area is in the central part of the state. Christianity was established here earlier than almost anywhere else in the world. In 52 AD, St Thomas the Apostle, or 'Doubting Thomas', is said to have landed on the Malabar Coast, where a church with carved Hindu-style columns supposedly dates from the 4th century AD. There have been Syrian Christians in Kerala since at least 190 AD, and a visitor at that time reported seeing a Hebrew copy of the Gospel of St Matthew. There are 16th century Syrian churches in Kottayam. When the Portuguese arrived here 500 years ago, they were more than a little surprised to find Christianity already established along the Malabar Coast, and more than a little annoyed that these Christians had never heard of the Pope.

inertia: mental and physical inactivity

Southern Kerala

THIRUVANANTHAPURAM (Trivandrum)
Pop. 854,000 Tel Area Code: 0471

Built over seven hills, Thiruvananthapuram (City of the Sacred Serpent) is as noisy, polluted and bustling as any other Indian city – many travellers find it a hot, noisy shock after a few days of relative peace and quiet on the beaches of Kerala. Away from the transport hubs and busy Mahatma Gandi (MG) Rd, Thiruvananthapuram has managed to retain some of the **ambience** characteristic of old Kerala: red-tiled roofs, narrow winding lanes, etc. – but this link to a more easy-going past is disappearing fast. The overwhelming image is of **frenetic** activity involved in the construction of concrete-box buildings and the widening of hopelessly congested roads.

Political and religious tensions are always simmering in this educated but poor populace. In the words of a cynical local, 'the only time we all get together is for the clashes'. The capital city is the logical place to vent one's spleen, and barely a day goes by when some group is not agitating its cause and adding to the noise on the dusty streets.

There are only a few 'sights' within the city, which can easily be seen in one or two days, so it makes sense to base yourself at Kovalam Beach, just 16km south, where you can enjoy a sea breeze and a cooling swim, and make short visits to the capital.

ambience: atmosphere
frenetic: frantic

Barbados and Malaysia

from Worldwide Holidays 2000 Tradewinds

Every year, thousands of tonnes of paper are used to create glossy holiday brochures. Millions of people spend hours looking at them, trying to decide where to go. The tour operators who are best at persuading people to travel with them stand to make enormous profits, so there are clear advantages to the art of persuasive writing!

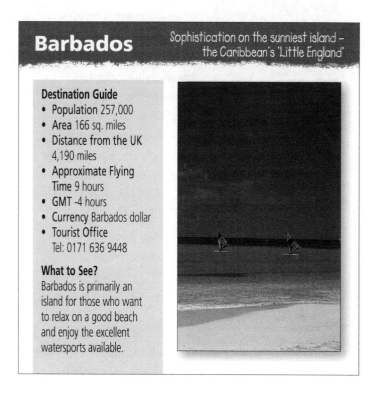

Barbados

Sophistication on the sunniest island – the Caribbean's 'Little England'

Destination Guide
- Population 257,000
- Area 166 sq. miles
- Distance from the UK 4,190 miles
- Approximate Flying Time 9 hours
- GMT -4 hours
- Currency Barbados dollar
- Tourist Office Tel: 0171 636 9448

What to See?
Barbados is primarily an island for those who want to relax on a good beach and enjoy the excellent watersports available.

Colonial Barbados – many old colonial houses and plantations when sugar ruled!

Bridgetown – the island capital and a great spot for good shopping and excellent fresh seafood around the picturesque marina. Quaint parliament buildings, St Michael's Cathedral, dating from 1831, and the Barbados Museum, once the military prison.

Atlantic Coast – is wild and rugged and merits at least a short visit. Steep, white headlands plunge down to the shore and you might be able to find a deserted cove somewhere.

Harrison's Cave – where a special tram will take you down through an exciting cavern of stalagmites and stalactites.

Welchman Hall Gully – is a vast tropical forest now running wild and once a spice plantation.

Flower Forest – offers some splendid views of the sea, as

A consistent favourite with British visitors, Barbados is an ideal introduction to the Caribbean. The most established in a chain of holiday havens, the island offers everything to entertain the visitor. It's known as Little England for its old colonial customs, which range from **unobtrusive** courtesy and colonnaded houses to afternoon tea and cricket whites. A more recent and perhaps more relevant **epithet** is 'the millionaire's playground' – for here is the widest range of watersports in the West Indies and an impressive list of land-based facilities including championship golf and floodlit tennis.

unobtrusive: does not draw attention to itself
epithet: a short phrase used to describe a characteristic

well as horticultural attractions from ginger lilies to cabbage palms.

Best Buys

Offering a wide choice, shopping in Barbados has the bonus of duty free establishments. Look for radios, cameras and Swiss watches, whilst typical handicraft items include reed place mats, jewellery made from seashells and ceramics.

Food and Drink

The essence of Caribbean cooking is based on natural produce – fish, shellfish, exotic fruits and vegetables, and a touch of spice. Spirits and wines are available everywhere, while each bartender has his own trade secret for a good rum punch.

Travel Wise

Many of the hotels have a dress code in the evening. The hotels are generally quiet at night although some nights there may be a local band.

In Bridgetown and the island's fashionable west coast resorts, there's an international atmosphere, with bars and restaurants to suit your every mood and nightlife varying from lively limbo to disco dancing. Along with local foresight and efficiency, Barbados has been blessed with many gifts of nature, among them the most temperate of climates. Beautiful beaches on her western shore are gently lapped by Caribbean waters, while to the east great breakers of Atlantic surf crash against the shore. A unique mix of colony and calypso, Barbados is the vital introduction to the Caribbean.

Malaysia

Beautiful beach resorts, lush forests and fascinating history

Destination Guide
- Population 17,756,000
- Area 127,320 sq miles
- Distance from the UK 6,550 miles
- Approximate Flying Time 13 hours
- GMT + 8 hours
- Currency Malaysian Ringgit
- Tourist Office Tel 0171 930 7932

What to See?
Kuala Lumpur – King's Palace, Parliament House and the bustle of Chinatown, shrine of a Hindu God, Batu caves.
Penang – Georgetown, Chinese temple of Kuan Yin Teng, colonial houses and traditional Muslim temples.
Langkawi – primarily islands for relaxation and beach combing with relatively little development.
Borneo – guardian fort, hillside temple, Mount Kinabalu, the highest peak between the Himalayas and New Guinea. State capital is Kota Kinabalu, with the beautiful resort of Tanjung Aru just 3 miles away.

Stretching south from Thailand to Singapore, with tiny islands anchored just off-shore, the Malaysian peninsula forms a beautiful barrier between the Indian Ocean and South China Sea. Famed for its Malay tigers and the endearing and endangered orang-utan, the country's greatest magnets for today's tourist are the sun-drenched beaches of lively resorts and the gentle pace of life around secluded island shores. Modern

Best Buys

Both Kuala Lumpur and Penang are centres for masterfully faked watches and designer jeans while something more typical such as puppets, wood carvings, silverwork and pewter can be found in the local handicraft shops. Batik is both hand and factory made and has a number of uses.

Food and Drink

Food in Malaysia represents a mix between Indian, Balinese and Chinese and is best sampled at one of the many food stalls for a true gastronomic adventure. Typical Malay dishes include satay while others are based on Hokkien (noodles), soya beans and coconut milk.

Travel Wise

Be very careful of weather conditions – each side of the peninsula has different rainy seasons (West: May–Sep, East: Nov–Feb). In Penang jellyfish can also be present at certain times of the year.

Malaysia is a rich **pot-pourri** of Asian cultures, peopled by Malay villagers, nomadic tribes, and large communities of Cantonese and Indian descent. In the cosmopolitan capital of Kuala Lumpur, you will discover temples, mosques and the delights of Chinatown.

The island of Penang boasts the largest butterfly farm in the world, and batik factories where you can watch the traditional art of printing cloth with wax and dyes. Both Penang and Langkawi offer a satisfying contrast between lively beach resorts and a quieter tropical paradise. There is, however, a unifying factor, a quality to be found in all Malaysians; it is the concept of 'senang' – contentment, comfort, ease of mind – and this is the atmosphere that all visitors to Malaysia will experience and carry with them for many years to come.

pot-pourri: mixture

Journey to Thailand

from The Real Beach *The Times* Website

As the Hollywood blockbuster *The Beach* opened in Britain, Dimitri Doganis recalled his own journey to Thailand where, like the hero of the film, he was at first seduced by the beauty of the surroundings and the hedonistic lifestyle. But he too saw the darker side of paradise when his friend was found dead.

Pickpockets and Thieues

Back Forward Stop Refresh Home Favorites History Search AutoFill Larger Smaller Print Mail Preferences

Address: http://www.

The real beach

The only clear memory I have of Koh Phangan is of the day I arrived. It was blisteringly hot as, just after noon, the longtail boat chugged through the waters of the Gulf of Thailand. Everything seemed to shimmer in the sun as the island rose like a mirage to greet us.

It was January 1990, I was 18 and travelling with my friend Leo; both of us were taking a year off before heading for university. We had heard about Phangan in London; everyone who had been to Thailand was talking about it.

We landed on Haad Rin beach, a thin strip of land with beaches on both sides – dubbed 'sunrise' and 'sunset' – separated by maybe 500 metres of forest and swamp. Leaving Leo with the bags, I followed a dirt track towards the other side of the peninsula. The whole island appeared to be silent and deserted.

As I walked through the coconut palms to the beach I came to a row of huts. On the back of the nearest one was a huge psychedelic mural that said 'Welcome to Tommy's Resort'. It was straight off a Sixties album cover. I stepped past the huts and on to a golden beach.

It was like a postcard from paradise. Strung out across the sand was a collection of the most beautiful people I had ever seen. Half of them were naked, the rest dressed in traveller chic – perfect tans, ethnic jewellery, Californian surfer T-shirts.

At one end of the beach there was a volleyball game; music was playing; They were an eclectic mix but seemed more like fully fledged hippy dropouts than middle-class kids on their way to university. I ran back to Leo, barely able to contain my excitement. 'I think we're going to like it here,' I said. It would be four months before we understood

Journey to Thailand

Address: http://www.

that what had at first seemed like heaven was in fact hell.

Haad Rin was cut off from the rest of the island – the only way in or out was by boat. It was a tiny fishing village that had been colonised by travellers and transformed into a tiny anarchic state. There were no police, or authorities.

There was a handful of bungalows whose owners sold Thai food, a disco called Casablancas, and there were two beaches.

The days would slide into each other, spent on the beach or in hammocks marvelling at the beauty of the place. There were no cars, no roads, no phones. The longer you were there, the more the outside world slipped away. Who you had been and where you had come from were easily forgotten. Then there were the parties.

I don't remember that much about the parties. The only thing that stays with me is sunrise. The beach looked east, and dawn was the climax of each party. As the sun rose above the horizon everyone faced out to sea to greet it, arms aloft. The magnetism of the

Address: http://www.

island was irresistible. The phrase 'I'm leaving tomorrow' would be greeted with hilarity because everyone knew that you would oversleep, be too stoned or think of something to put off the return to reality. The in-joke was that this was the 'Hotel California' of the Eagles song – 'You can check out any time you want / but you can never leave'.

And as I got used to island life it began to dawn on me that all was not as it had seemed. Some of the people who had seemed mystical and laid-back were just junkies. The nice man selling pineapple slices on the beach was also selling heroin. The cool dudes who were never going home were actually failures who could not hack it in the real world. This paradise had a dark side. There were strange stories about bodies washing up on the beach. About suicides and overdoses, corpses being burnt in the swamp. The asylum on the neighbouring island was filling up with travellers. After a while you would hear too many rumours to be able to dismiss them all.

Our presence on the island – and our money – was destroying the paradise we had

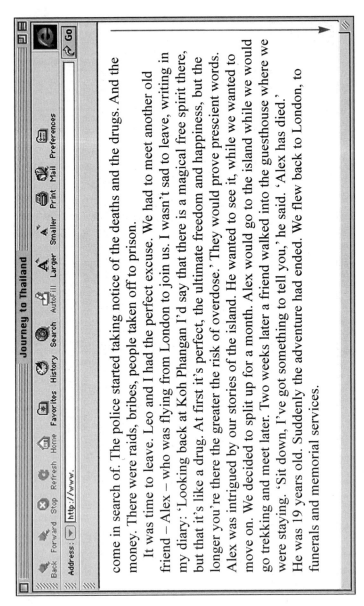

come in search of. The police started taking notice of the deaths and the drugs. And the money. There were raids, bribes, people taken off to prison.

It was time to leave. Leo and I had the perfect excuse. We had to meet another old friend – Alex – who was flying from London to join us. I wasn't sad to leave, writing in my diary: 'Looking back at Koh Phangan I'd say that there is a magical free spirit there, but that it's like a drug. At first it's perfect, the ultimate freedom and happiness, but the longer you're there the greater the risk of overdose.' They would prove prescient words. Alex was intrigued by our stories of the island. He wanted to see it, while we wanted to move on. We decided to split up for a month. Alex would go to the island while we would go trekking and meet later. Two weeks later a friend walked into the guesthouse where we were staying. 'Sit down, I've got something to tell you,' he said. 'Alex has died.'

He was 19 years old. Suddenly the adventure had ended. We flew back to London, to funerals and memorial services.

Alex's death was a mystery. The post mortem suggested a drugs overdose, but was inconclusive. His money and credit cards had been stolen, and we heard rumours from travellers about an attack on a young Englishman. Was this Alex? All the horror stories we had heard were not just evidence of wild times in a mad place. They were tragedies involving sons and brothers of loving families.

I knew that it was our stories of parties in paradise that had prompted Alex to go. And I knew that if we had not split up my friend would still be alive. It took me ten years to go back. Last autumn I returned to Thailand to make a documentary – *The Real Beach* – for Channel 4 about backpackers in paradise, prompted by the film of Alex Garland's novel *The Beach*. It seemed like an opportunity to make sense of everything that had happened a decade ago.

On my return I finally discovered what had happened to Alex, and it was pretty much what we had imagined. Finding out was like a weight being lifted off my shoulders. It has left me giddy with a relief that I find difficult to explain.

Thousands more people have passed through it since I was first there. Koh Phangan has become somewhere to go for a wild two-week holiday as well as a backpacker destination. The island is in every guidebook, there are thousands of rooms and bungalows filled to bursting, and what used to be a tiny village now boasts roads, telephones and e-mail cafés.

But the people there are the same types, having much the same experiences that we had. At 28, I felt old. Ten years ago I thought we had found paradise. It was brilliant and beautiful, and is still the best time I've ever had. But it was dark and terrible and I wish we had never gone there. Now that some of the ghosts are fading, I think my experiences were about coming of age, more than about Thailand. The important thing about places such as Koh Phangan is not what we hope to find there. It's what we bring with us.

The Real Beach was broadcast on Channel 4, Saturday 12 February 2000

Activities

An American student arrives in the UK

1 Use a table like the one below to note down the things that Bill Bryson says were good and bad about his arrival in England.

Good	NOT good!
I liked having an English town all to myself	I couldn't find anywhere to stay

2 As a whole class, discuss the following:

- What points does Bill Bryson make about England and English attitudes?
- Compare the attitudes of the owner of the guest house and the man with the dog. How do they differ? Are these 'typical' English characters?
- Are we meant to take Bill Bryson's observations seriously, or is he just being entertaining? Explain your answer.

3 Have you ever arrived somewhere that is new to you such as a new school, house, country or town?

- Brainstorm some words and phrases that could describe your feelings and thoughts when arriving. There are some examples in the box below.

| unfamiliar | threatening | enigmatic | weird |
| in the dark | vague about | unknown quantity | |

- Share these with other people in your class.
- Write a description of arriving at a new place. Use your word list to help you.

4 Now look at question 1 on page 79.

Travels in Egypt

1 Imagine you are part of the BBC film crew with Michael Palin. Write a diary of what happens to him in Alexandria, Cairo and at the Pyramids. The account should be factual – do not put in any thoughts/feelings that he describes in his diary. The first entry has been done for you.

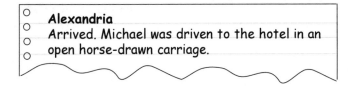

Alexandria
Arrived. Michael was driven to the hotel in an open horse-drawn carriage.

2 Now compare your diary entry with the extract. How does it differ? What feelings, comments and comparisons does the writer use to bring his journey alive? Discuss your findings with the rest of your group.

3 Make a list of words and phrases the writer uses to describe the noise of Egypt. Each member of the group can select one or more words or phrases to create a **sound poem** illustrating the sounds and cries of Egypt. For example:

'You are Michael Caine!'
blowing horns
call to prayer
traffic noise
donkeys
goats

4 Now look at question 1 on page 79.

Outdoor Excitement in Switzerland

1 These activities appeal to readers' sense of adventure.

- Why do people like to do scary things?
- What is the scariest activity any of your class has ever taken part in?
- Which of the activities would you like to have a go at? Which of them would you never want to try? Why?

2 Look at the symbols and key on page 50 and how they appear on each extract. Which are marked as the most exciting and dangerous (adrenalin driver)? Do you agree? If not, which would you have chosen? Give reasons for your answer.

3 How do the writers persuade readers to take part in the activities they offer? Write down phrases or sentences in which they:

- make promises:
  a you will impress your family and friends
  b you will have spectacular thrills
  c you will be successful
- challenge your courage
- emphasise the expertise of the instructors.

4 Select one of the activities listed. Imagine you have taken part in it. With reference to the symbols listed in the article, write a diary entry, a letter or an e-mail to a friend describing the activity and your sensations on doing it.

5 Now look at question 1 on page 79.

Kerala and Trivandrum

1 Imagine that you are planning a trip to Kerala. Use a table like the one below to make notes on things you would like to do, and things you would rather avoid.

Things to do:	Things to avoid:
Take a boat trip on the Coastal lagoons	political demonstrations

2 Using your notes, write a diary of a five-day visit to Kerala. You may wish to start your diary as follows:

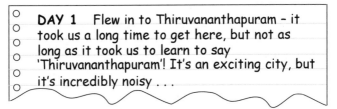

DAY 1   Flew in to Thiruvananthapuram – it took us a long time to get here, but not as long as it took us to learn to say 'Thiruvananthapuram'! It's an exciting city, but it's incredibly noisy . . .

3 Using the information in the extract, design a website or page for Kerala. Use the following headings and find or draw images you would use to illustrate it.

- General information (maps, statistics, festivals)
- History
- Religion
- Highlights for visitors
- Thiruvananthapuram

Remember to choose only the most important pieces of information for your site. You don't want it to appear too 'cluttered'. If you'd like a model to work to, try looking at http://www.kerala.com.

4 Now look at question 1 on page 79.

Barbados and Malaysia

1 What is the purpose of the extracts on Barbados and Malaysia? Who are their intended audience? Support your answers with evidence from the texts.

2 The writers of the extracts tempt visitors with the promise of wonderful things to see and do.

   a Complete a table like the one below that shows how the writer uses adjectives and nouns to tempt people to go on holiday in Malaysia.

adjective	noun	adjective	noun
beautiful	barrier	endearing (and endangered)	orang-utan
sun-drenched	beaches	lively	resorts

   b Now draw up a similar table for Barbados.

3 In groups, discuss your list of adjectives. How effective is each one? In the blank spaces, write down adjectives that the group decides would be as effective as, or more effective than, each adjective used in the extract.

4 What reasons do the extracts give you for going to Barbados and Malaysia? Complete lists like the ones below.

Reasons to go to Barbados   **Reasons to go to Malaysia**
Wide range of watersports   Largest butterfly farm

5 Work in pairs. **A** wants a holiday. **B** is a travel agent. **B** has to persuade **A** to buy the holiday in Barbados.

   A I'd like a holiday, please.
   B I've got the perfect place for you. Barbados!

When you have finished, change roles. This time **B** has to persuade **A** to take the holiday in Malaysia.

Discuss the effectiveness of your role plays. How did you persuade the 'Customer' to buy your holiday?

6 Now look at question 1 on page 79.

Journey to Thailand

1 Think of a title for each paragraph (numbering each one) that says what it is about, and make a list of them. Then answer the following questions:

- How does Dimitri Doganis tall the story of his stay on Koh Phangan?
- If he had been writing a book about his experiences, in what ways might he have told the story differently? Explain your answer.

2 The author makes a strong contrast between the wonderful and not-so-good aspects of life on the island. Make lists of the advantages and disadvantages of life on Koh Phangan under the following headings.

Brilliant and beautiful	Dark and terrible
Great parties	Someone died of heroin overdose
Beautiful people	Nobody ever left

3 The film *The Beach* is about an 'earthly paradise' where life turns sour. Is it possible for life on Earth to be perfect? Imagine you are marooned with a group of people on an island which has everything needed to support life (including minerals for building machines if required).

- Write down ten things that you would need to do to ensure that everyone could live on the island in peace and harmony.
- Share your list with the rest of the group. From all the ideas and rules put forward by everyone in the group, choose ten that everyone agrees on – if you can!

4 Have you ever been in a situation where something you thought was going to be harmless fun has turned out to be a nightmare? Write a report about your experience as a warning to anyone who may become caught in the same trap.

5 Now look at question 1 on page 79.

Comparing texts

1 Each piece of travel writing has a particular purpose. The
language and **structure** of a piece of writing helps get this
purpose across to the reader. For each extract in this
section use a format like the one on page 194 (see a
completed example on page 196) to write a report on how
these pieces of travel writing achieve their effect.

2 Choose an extract from this section which is concerned
with selling holidays. Compare it with one that is giving an
impression of a country to people who have never been
there and may never be able to visit it.

Look back at the reports you have completed on the **text
type**, **language**, **tone**, **narrator**, **address** and **period** of the
extracts. Use these to help show how the writers have used
different approaches in order to achieve their purpose.

3 Choose one of the extracts below and rewrite it in the
style suggested. Make sure you use the features that you
have identified as belonging to that style.

Extract	Rewrite in the style of
Kerala and Trivandrum (pages 56–60) (concentrating on the travel information)	→ **Barbados and Malaysia** (pages 61–65) Write a holiday brochure for Kerala.
Journey to Thailand (pages 66–72) Arrival on the island to the description of greeting the sunrise (page 68)	→ **An American student arrives in the UK** (pages 61–65) Use Bill Bryson's ironic style to show the downside of this island 'paradise' from the outset.

4 Choose one of the styles in this section to write about a
place that you have visited, or that you have read about or

researched. Remember to include the features that you have studied for that style, and to:

- **use telling descriptions** – either to entice the visitor – 'beautiful beaches . . . gently lapped by Caribbean waters' (*Barbados* page 63) – or to describe the reality – 'sleeping, low-lit streets threaded with fog' (Bill Bryson, page 40)
- **make sure that your purpose and audience are clear**: are you using lots of adjectives to make the place you have chosen sound attractive to visitors? or are you giving an impression of the place to someone who has never seen it?
- **choose your narrative viewpoint carefully** – will it be more effective for you to say: 'I went there, I did this' (first person); 'You should go there, you should do this' (second person); He/she/they went there and did this' (third person)?

You should **structure your work** with an arresting opening, interesting development and an ending that sums up your intentions in writing the article: for example, 'Barbados is an ideal introduction to the Caribbean' (*Barbados,* page 62) or 'the important thing about places such as Koh Phangan is not what we hope to find there. It's what we bring with us' (*Journey to Thailand*, page 72).

Make sure that you use:

- headings
- paragraphs
- complete sentences.

Section 3
Cities

Cities are places where large numbers of people have come together to live and work. This is their common link. However, no two cities are alike. Each of the world's cities has its own personality, history and culture.

In this section, travel writers examine cities, their inhabitants and their lifestyles.

The origins of Australia's greatest city
from Sydney
by Jan Morris

Sydney is Australia's largest city. Its Opera House and harbour bridge are world-famous landmarks and it was chosen to host the 2000 Olympic Games. But Sydney wasn't always regarded so highly.

In this extract, Jan Morris tell us how the city has changed over time and gives us a series of 'snapshots' of Sydney and its people.

On a Sunday afternoon in late summer two elderly people in white linen hats, husband and wife without a doubt, and amiably married for thirty or forty years, stand at the parkland tip of Bradley's Head on the northern shore of Sydney Harbour in Australia. She wears a flowery cotton dress, he is in white shorts, though not of the very abbreviated kind known to Australia as stubbies. Both husband and wife have binoculars slung around their necks, both have sheets of white paper in their hands – lists of bird species, perhaps? – and even as we watch them, with a sudden excitement they raise their binoculars as one, and look eagerly out across the water.

At such a time – Sunday arvo in the Australian vernacular – Sydney Harbour is crowded. It is a kind of boat-jam out there. Hundreds upon hundreds of yachts skim, loiter, tack and race each other in the sunshine, yachts slithery and majestic, yachts traditional and experimental, solitary or in bright flotillas. Stolid ferry-boats plod their way through the confusion. The Manly hydrofoil sweeps by. An occasional freighter passes on its way to the Pyrmont piers. A warship makes for the ocean. Distantly amplified guide-book voices sound from excursion cruisers, or there may be a boom of heavy rock from a party boat somewhere. And presently into our line of sight there burst the 18-footers of the Sydney Flying Squadron, which is what our dedicated pensioners have really been waiting for – not bower-birds or whistle-ducks, but furiously fast racing yachts. They came into our vision like thunderbolts. Dear God, how those boats move! They look perfectly prepared to sink anything that gets in their way.

Romantics like to think that the 18-footers have developed from the hell-for-leather cutters of rum-smugglers, and in evolving forms they have certainly been a beloved and familiar facet of this city's life for more than a century. Behind them, in the harbour **mélange**, we may be able to identify a smallish ferry-boat pursuing them up the harbour: this is a beloved and familiar facet too, for unless it has lately been raided by plainclothes policemen, its passengers include a complement of punters, elderly people many of them, who go out each

mélange: mixture

Sunday to place their illegal bets on the flying yachts before them – and some of whom, we need not doubt, were once themselves those sweating young toughs, brown as nuts, agile as cats, driving so tremendously before the harbour wind.

I choose to start a book about Sydney with this scene because I think it includes many of the elements which have created this city, and which sustain its character still. The glory of the harbour, the showy **hedonism** of its Sunday afternoon, the brutal force of the 18-footers, the mayhem aboard the gambler's ferry-boat, the white-hatted old lovers – the mixture of the homely, the illicit, the beautiful, the nostalgic, the ostentatious, the formidable and the quaint, all bathed in sunshine and somehow impregnated with a fragile sense of passing generations, passing time, presents to my mind a proper introduction to the feel of the place.

Books about Sydney are innumerable, but they are mostly guide-books, works of civic history or social analyses, and they have nearly all been written by Australians. No foreigner has tried to write a full-scale study or evocation, and this is not surprising; it is only in the last years of the twentieth century that Sydney has joined the company of the great **metropoles**. To inhabit a 'world-class' city was always an aspiration of Sydney people, but it took them two centuries to achieve it.

Of course everyone had long had an idea of the city – if the world thought of Australia at all it generally thought of Sydney. Its harbour was popularly ranked for beauty with those of San Francisco, Rio de Janeiro, Hong Kong, Naples, Vancouver and Istanbul. Its sad origins as an eighteenth-century penal colony exerted an unhealthy

---

hedonism: pleasure-seeking
metropoles: capital cities

fascination, and fostered many a gibe about criminal tendencies. Its accent was a gift to humorists. Its harbour bridge had been one of the world's best-known structures since 1932, and since 1966 its Opera House had provided one of the most familiar of all architectural shapes. Bondi Beach was an **archetypal** pleasure beach, the quarter called King's Cross was an international **synonym** for Rest and Recreation of the racier kind, and the interminable suburbs of Sydney, so vast that in built-up area this city is twice as large as Beijing and six times as large as Rome, had long figured in traveller's tales as an epitome of urban error. As for the people of Sydney, they had impressed themselves upon the universal fancy as an **esoteric** sub-species of Briton – sunburnt, healthy, loud, generous, **misogynist**, beery, lazy, capable, racist and entertaining, strutting along beaches in bathing-caps, carrying banners, exchanging **badinage** or war memoirs in raw colonial slang, barracking unfortunate Englishmen at cricket matches they nearly always won.

It was a vivid image, but it was essentially provincial. Sydney was thought of, by and large, as second rate – far from the centres of power, art or civil manners, of uncouth beginnings and ungentlemanly presence. Throughout the twentieth century, visiting writers, mostly British, had been variously condescending and abusive about the city. At the turn of the century Beatrice Webb the radical thought it chiefly notable for its bad taste: its people were aggressive in manner and blatant in dress, while its Mayor and Aldermen were one and all 'heavy common persons'. In 1923 D. H. Lawrence, who spent

---

archetypal: original, model

synonym: word that means the same as another word

esoteric: secret, strange

misogynist: someone who dislikes women

badinage: backchat

two days in the city, declared it no more than a substitute London, made in five minutes – 'as margarine is a substitute for butter'. Robert Morley the actor, in 1949, thought the city misnamed – 'why didn't they call it Bert?' Neville Cardus the music critic, in 1952, said it was just like Manchester, except that the harbour was at the bottom of Market Street instead of the river Irwell. Denis Brogan the political philosopher, in 1958, thought the old-fashioned ladies' underwear on display in the big stores revealed 'all too plainly the acceptance of a non-competitive mediocrity'. 'By God, what a site!' cried Clough Williams-Ellis the architect in the 1950s. 'By man, what a mess!' And nobody was ruder that I was, when I first went to Sydney in the early 1960s. It was, then, no more than a harbour surrounded by suburbs – its origins unsavoury, its temper coarse, its organisation slipshod, the expression of its society ladies 'steely, scornful, accusatory and **plebeian**, as though they are expecting you (which heaven forbid) to pinch their tight-corseted behinds'. It was five full years before the last letter of complaint reached me from down under.

The world turns; societies, like authors, age and mature; today Sydney really is, by general consent, one of the great cities of the world. Its population, though still predominantly British and Irish in stock, has been alleviated by vast influxes of immigrants from the rest of Europe and from Asia. Modern communications and the shifts of historical consequence mean that it is no longer on the distant perimeter of affairs, but strategically placed upon the frontier of twentieth-century change, the Pacific Rim. Its prickly old **parochialism** has been softened by a perceptible ability to laugh at itself, and a flood of Sydney talent has been unleashed upon us all, greatly changing

---

plebeian: low-born
parochialism: narrow, limited outlook

perceptions of the city. When in 1988 the bicentennial of European settlement in Australia was spectacularly celebrated around the harbour, with fireworks and operas and tall ships, a new version of Sydney, resplendent, festive and powerful, was once and for all stamped upon the general imagination.

Back to Bradley's Head; and as we watch the 18-footers storm out of view, that crystal light and smother of trees is all around us, and the skyscrapers look back at us from over the water. And to add to the authenticity of the scene, now it turns out that our friends in the white hats have a little money on the boats too. 'Betting?' they say with poker faces. 'We don't know the meaning of the word.' But those papers in their hands are race cards, not bird-spotting charts, and when Xerox and Prudential disappear behind the trees they carefully hasten down the woodland track around the point, the better to follow their fancies. The contest lasts for another couple of hours, and sends the boats twice scudding up and down the harbour along courses dictated by the weather; thus making sure that whether it is the dry west wind that is blowing that day, or the maverick they call a Southerly Buster, or a humid nor'-easter out of the Tasman Sea, in one direction or another the Flying Squadron is sure to go pounding through, as our old enthusiasts might say, like a Bondi tram.

Kiev and the KGB

from Among the Russians
by Colin Thubron

Before the collapse of the Soviet Union, Russia was a closed society. During the 1960s and 1970s very few Western visitors were allowed into Russia. Tourists were practically unheard of. The few who did visit were only allowed to do so as part of closely-supervised package tours.

However, a writer called Colin Thubron did the unthinkable. Travelling on his own, he drove his battered Morris Marina thousands of miles from the Baltic to the Black Sea, through the heart of the Soviet Union.

For much of his trip, it seemed that the KGB, the dreaded Russian secret police, took little interest in Thubron. But when he reached Kiev, the capital of the Ukraine, all that suddenly changed . . .

For several weeks I had visited nobody controversial and my vigilance had slackened. But that evening I overheard an assistant at the hotel's **Intourist** telephone-desk. Her tone was tense and **deferential**. She was answering questions. 'A lone British tourist? . . . yes . . . with his own car? . . . He arrived at 5.30 . . .'

As she put down the receiver I asked, still untroubled: 'Did somebody want me?'

She jumped. 'You're Mr Thubron? . . . Yes . . . They, we . . .' She was blushing, staring down and scrabbling furiously with her papers. When she looked up again her

---

Intourist: the state-run tourist agency
deferential: humble

voice was loud and bright: 'If there's anything you want, we're absolutely at your service.'

I took a mental note of the car number-plates behind the hotel, and that evening it was one of these which framed itself in my mirror as I drove south into the suburbs: Kiev 75–86. Once it had gauged my speed, the white Volga saloon lingered back in a way which I was soon to recognise, tucked behind a lorry four cars behind. I might have shaken it off – it assumed I was unaware of it. But by now I was worried. I had no idea why I was wanted. Had they traced me back to meetings with **dissidents** in Moscow or Leningrad? I didn't know. Every minute or two the white shadow in my mirror would ease out as if to pass its covering lorry, then slide back. Once, in distraction, I overshot some red traffic-lights, and the Volga accelerated and did the same. A policeman tried to flag it down. It took no notice and swerved in close behind me. I saw a short, dark man seated in front, and a thin, fair driver. They fell back again instantly, concealed behind a truck.

For the next four days I was followed everywhere. I came to recognise the techniques of the white Volgas (they were always white), sheltered by lorries a hundred yards behind me. Highly trained, they behaved in ways which were eventually so recognisable that by the fifth day I would pick them out at a glance. But by now I was riddled with nerves. I was afraid above all that my travel notes, compressed into the form of an illegible diary, would be discovered and taken away. Isolated, I began to partake in the condemnation of my silent spectators. I began to feel deeply, inherently guilty. A single friend might have saved me from this, but I didn't have one. I understood now the precious intensity of personal relationships among the dissidents. Because around me,

---

dissidents: people who are known to oppose the government

as around them, the total, all-eclipsing Soviet world, which renders any other world powerless and far away, had become profoundly, morally hostile.

In the long, carpetless halls of the hotel, the walled-up faces of waiting men and the sunny voices of the Intourist girls became the scenario of nightmare. I began to behave guiltily. For a whole day I **incarcerated** myself in my room, illegibly writing up and disguising notes. I searched for a bugging device in vain; I did not dare even curse to myself. Then I wondered if I had implicated anybody else, and decided to destroy my list of Russian addresses and telephone numbers. The irony was that there was no person on it, dissident or other, who did not feel passionately for his country's good. But I could not decide how to destroy this paper. The problem became tortuous. If I shredded the list into my waste-paper basket, it might be reconstructed. If I went into the passage, the eyes of the **concierges** followed me; and all the public rooms were heavy with scrutiny. If I went out, I would be followed. So, like a cunning schoolboy, I burnt the list in my lavatory.

'Fire!' A fat laundry-maid burst in. 'Fire! Where's all this smoke from? Fire!' She had a blotched, **porcine** face which sloped neckless into her body. I stared at her with pure hate.

A young concierge appeared behind. Her gaze hardened and flew round the room.

'What's this?'

'I've been smoking.'

'Only smoking?'

'Yes.'

---

incarcerated: buried
concierges: female caretakers who sit at a desk on each floor of a Russian hotel **porcine**: pig-like

I felt angry, shaken by my own lie. The concierge marched back past her desk and descended the elevator. I imagined myself under inquisition, trying to clear myself. I never smoke. But in one corner of the stairway landing stood an ash-bin where I found three cigarette-stubs. As if participating in some third-rate thriller, I took them back to my room, lit them to foil forensic tests, and left them in the lavatory. Then I walked downstairs and out into the sun, refusing to look behind me. I was shaking.

When I returned to my hotel, I knew that something was wrong. The comfortable old concierge who had taken over duty on my floor, and who had previously shown a **maternal benignity**, now gaped at me with horror.

My room, in my absence, had been searched. It had been done near-perfectly, everything repositioned almost precisely as it was. Only by the pinpoint siting of several objects before I left, and by the insertion in notebooks of tiny threads now dislodged, did I realise that everything I possessed – letters, clothes, wallet, books, documents – had been removed, scrutinised and fastidiously replaced.

But my diary was in my pocket, and my address-list ashes down the lavatory.

Next day, Colin Thubron drove to the border. He was followed all the way. He was forced to wait for several hours at the border post, while his belongings were searched and his car was taken apart piece by piece.

The KGB officers were unable to discover any evidence of wrongdoing. In spite of his fears, they returned all the author's property – even the coded diary from which he later wrote his book.

---

maternal benignity: motherly kindness

London parks

from The Eyewitness Guide to London
by Michael Leapman

London's parks are one of the capital's best features.
They're big, there's lots of room for a kick about with a
football, there's usually a game of street hockey going
on, and you don't have to pay to get in. There are also
more official things to see and do, as the *Eyewitness
Guide* explains.

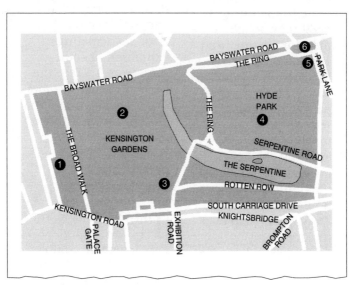

Map showing the locations described in the guide

Kensington Palace[1]

HALF OF THIS SPACIOUS palace is used as lavish royal apartments: Princess Margaret has a base here. The other half, which includes the 18th century state rooms, is open to the public. When William III and his wife Mary came to the throne in 1689 they bought a mansion, dating from 1605, and commissioned *Christopher Wren to convert it into a royal palace. He created separate suites of rooms for the king and queen, and today visiting members of public use the queen's entrance – note the William and Mary monogram over the door.

The palace has seen some important royal events. In 1714 Queen Anne died here from a fit of apoplexy brought on by over-eating and, on 20 June 1837, Princess Victoria of Kent was woken at 5a.m. to be told that her uncle William IV had died and she was now queen – the start of her 64-year reign.

Highlights of the palace are the finely decorated state rooms and, on the ground floor, a fascinating exhibition of court dress from 1760 to the present, which includes dresses belonging to the Queen, Queen Mother and Queen Mary.

Kensington Gardens[2]

THE FORMER GROUNDS of Kensington Palace became a public park in 1841 and now merge imperceptibly

---

*Christopher Wren: A famous architect, best known for designing St Paul's Cathedral

into Hyde Park to the east. The gardens are full of charm, starting with Sir George Frampton's statue (1912) of J. M. Barrie's fictional ***Peter Pan**, the boy who never grew up, playing his pipes to the bronze fairies and animals that cling to the column below him. Often surrounded by parents, nannies and their charges, the statue stands near the west bank of the Serpentine, not far from where Harriet, wife of the poet Percy Bysshe Shelley, drowned herself in 1816.

Just north of here are the ornamental fountains and statues, including Jacob Epstein's *Rima*, at the lake's head. George Frederick Watts's statue of a muscular horse and rider, *Physical Energy*, stands to the south. Not far away are a summer house designed by William Kent in 1735 and the Serpentine Gallery. The Round Pond, created in 1728 just east of the palace, is often packed with model boats navigated by children and older enthusiasts. In winter it is occasionally fit for skating. In the north, near Lancaster Gate, is a dogs' cemetery, started in 1880 by the Duke of Cambridge while mourning one of his pets.

Serpentine Gallery[3]

IN THE SOUTHEAST corner of Kensington Gardens is the Serpentine Gallery, which houses temporary exhibitions of contemporary

*Peter Pan: J. M. Barrie's book was a smash hit in 1904 and is still a firm favourite. It has given rise to many books and films.

painting and sculpture. The building is a former tea pavilion built in 1912; exhibits often spill out into the surrounding park. Its tiny bookshop has a remarkable stock of art books.

Hyde Park[4]

THE ANCIENT Manor of Hyde was part of the lands of Westminster Abbey seized by Henry VIII at the Dissolution of the Monasteries in 1536. It has remained a royal park ever since. Henry used it for hunting but James I opened it to the public in the early 17th century, and it became one of the city's most prized public spaces. The Serpentine, an artificial lake used for boating and bathing, was created when Caroline, George II's queen, dammed the flow of the Westbourne River in 1730.

In its time the park has been a venue for duelling, horse racing, highwaymen, political demonstrations, music (Mick Jagger and Luciano Pavarotti have each had a concert here) and parades. The 1851 Exhibition was held here in a vast glass palace.

The aristocracy drove their carriages on the outer roads.

Speaker's Corner[5]

IN 1872 A LAW made it legal to assemble an audience and address them on whatever topic you chose; since then this corner of Hyde Park has become the established venue for budding orators and a fair number of eccentrics. It is well worth spending time here on a Sunday: speakers from fringe groups and one-member political parties reveal their plans for the betterment of mankind while the assembled onlookers heckle them without mercy.

Marble Arch[6]

J OHN NASH designed the arch in 1827 as the main entrance to Buckingham Palace. It was, however, too narrow for the grandest coaches and was moved here in 1851. Now, only senior members of the Royal Family and one of the royal artillery regiments are allowed to pass under it.

The arch stands near the site of the old Tyburn gallows (marked by a plaque), where until 1783 the city's most notorious criminals were hanged in front of crowds of bloodthirsty spectators.

Nightlife in Beirut

from Holidays in Hell

by P. J. O'Rourke

The American journalist and foreign correspondent P. J. O'Rourke has made something of a speciality of writing about the world's trouble spots, using 'the techniques of humour to report on real news events'. He says: 'I was curious about the trouble man causes himself and which he could presumably quit causing himself at the drop of a hat or, anyway, a gun.'

In 1984 he went to Beirut, the capital of the Lebanon, with a less than serious brief to investigate its tourist industry. At the time the country was in the grip of a savage civil war. The combatants belonged to various Islamic and Christian sects, encouraged by Israel and Syria. From being a peaceful and prosperous country, the Lebanon was reduced to a dangerous shambles and Beirut to rubble – not really the best city for a visit, unless you're P. J. O'Rourke . . .

West Beirut can be toured on foot. You'll find the city is full of surprises – a sacking of the Saudi embassy because of long lines for visas to Mecca, for instance, or shelling of the lower town by an unidentified gunboat or car bombs several times a day. Renaults are the favoured vehicles. Avoid double-parked Le Cars. Do not, however, expect the population to be moping around glassy eyed. There's lots of jewellery and make-up and the silliest Italian designer jeans on earth. The streets are jammed. Everyone's very busy, though not exactly working. They're rushing from one place to another in order to sit around drinking hundreds of tiny cups of Turkish coffee and chat at the top of their lungs. The entire economy is fuelled, as far as I could see, by everyone selling cartons of smuggled Marlboros to each other.

The **Bois de Pins**, planted in the 1600s to protect Beirut from encroaching sand dunes, had all its foliage blown off by Israeli jets and looks like a phone-pole farm. The Place des Martyrs, so-called because eleven nationalists were hanged there by the Turks in 1915, is right on the **Green Line** and now all that much more aptly named. Most of the buildings on the **Corniche** have literally been face-lifted. The old American Embassy is here, in the same state as US Middle East policy. The British Embassy down the street is completely draped in anti-bomb nets imported from Belfast. Hotel Row was ravaged at the beginning of the civil war in 1975. The high-rise Holiday Inn is a delight to the eye. Who, when travelling around the earth faced with endless Holiday Inns has not fantasised blowing one to flinders? The National Museum is bricked up and surrounded with tanks – no nagging sense of cultural obligation to tour this historical treasure trove. I couldn't find the Great Mosque at all.

A surprising lot of Beirut stands, however. A building with a missing storey here, a lot with a missing building there, shattered this next to untouched that – all the usual ironies of war except with great restaurants.

The Summerland Hotel, on the beach in the ruined south suburbs, has good hamburgers. The wealthy Muslims, including Shiites, go here. Downtown on the Corniche you can lunch at the St George's Hotel, once

---

Bois de Pins: a plantation of pine trees

Green Line: a (theoretical) peace line separating Muslim West Beirut from Christian East Beirut

the Corniche: seafront road

Beirut's best. The hotel building is now a burned shell, but the pool club is still open. You can go waterskiing here, even during the worst fighting.

I asked the bartender at the pool club, 'Don't the waterskiers worry about sniper fire?'

'Oh, no, no, no,' he said, 'snipers are mostly armed with automatic weapons – these are not very accurate.'

Down the quay, **pristine** among the ruins, Chez Temporal serves excellent food. A short but careful walk through a heavily armed **Druse** neighbourhood brings you to Le Grenier, once a jet-set mob scene, now a quiet hideaway with splendid native dishes. Next door there's first-rate Italian fare at Quo Vadis. Be sure to tip the man who insists, at gunpoint, on guarding your car.

Spaghetteria is a favourite with the foreign press. The Italian specials are good, and there's a spectacular view of military patrols and night-time skirmishing along the beach front. Sit near the window if you feel lucky.

The Commodore also has restaurants. These are recommended during fighting. The Commodore always manages to get food delivered no matter what the situation outdoors.

Night-life begins late in Beirut. Cocktail hour at the Commodore is eight p.m., when US editors and network executives are safely at lunch (there's a seven hour time difference). The Commodore is strictly neutral territory with only one rule. No guns at the bar. All sorts of raffish characters hang about, expatriates from Palestine, Libya and Iran, officers **in mufti** from both sides of the Lebanese Army, and combatants of other stripes. I overheard one black Vietnam veteran loudly describe to

---

pristine: untouched, spotless
Druse: an Islamic sect that believes the Caliph al-Hakim to be the final incarnation of God
in mufti: out of uniform

two British girls how he teaches orthodox Muslim women to fight with knives. And there are diplomats, **spooks** and dealers in gold, arms and other things. At least that's what they seem to be. No one exactly announces his occupation – except the journalists, of course.

Dinner, if anyone remembers to have it, is at ten or so. People go out in groups. It's not a good idea to be alone and blonde after dark. Kidnapping is the one great innovation of the Lebanese civil war. And Reuters correspondent, Johnathan Wright, had disappeared thus on his way to the Bekáa Valley a few days before I arrived.

If nabbed, make as much noise as possible. Do not get in anyone's car. If forced in, attack the driver. At least this is what I'm told.

Be **circumspect** when driving at night. Other cars should be given a wide berth. Flick headlights off and on to indicate friendly approach. Turn on the dome light when arriving at checkpoints. Militiamen will fire a couple of bursts in your direction if they want you to slow down.

---

spooks: spies
circumspect: cautious

48 hours in Tel Aviv

from *The Guardian* by Mark Espiner

Reporter Mark Espiner describes the Israeli capital as having 'the edge of Belfast, the spirit of Rio and the 24-hour attitude of New York' ...

48 hours in Tel Aviv
A short break guide to Israel's capital

'It's the Russians, they've changed this city.' The cab driver taking me from the airport to my hotel looked disapprovingly at what he said were Russian prostitutes working on the street. 'You know, it isn't just the pimping and gambling that they have brought with them – they've put me out of a job, too. I have been forced to drive this taxi. I'm a pianist, but so many Russian pianists have come here now, I just can't get the work.'

His slender fingers spun the wheel, swerving the car in a u-turn to drop me at the door of my hotel. 'Russians aside,' he said, pocketing my tip and handing me my bag, 'welcome to the city that never sleeps.'

With a two-hour delay at Heathrow, an interview with El Al airline's security that would have put **Mossad** to shame (I wasn't special, they do it to everyone, apparently) and the anti-Russian taxi ride behind me, I wasn't

Mossad: Israeli military intelligence

quite ready for the non-sleeping city.

From my hotel room on the 16th floor, I surveyed the bright lights of Tel Aviv's high-rise skyline and phoned my friend Elan to tell him I had arrived and was going to bed. It was 11.45 p.m. I apologised for calling so late, but he cut me short. 'You're in Tel Aviv. Let's get a drink. It's a good one, it's a lovely one.' I had forgotten two things about Elan: his infectious enthusiasm and the fact that he said, 'It's a good one, it's a lovely one' at the end of every sentence.

On the way to the bar, he threw the sights of the city at me with the keen eye of the film-maker that he is: the street we were driving down, he said, was one of the first built in Tel Aviv at the beginning of the century –

they built this city on sand in 1906, you know. These houses on Rothschild Avenue – super chic modernist abodes – are all **Bauhaus** designs, built by emigrés in the 20s. Good ones, lovely ones.

That over there, with a raft of candles and soldiers standing by, is the exact spot where **Rabin** was assassinated. This corner is where Saddam Hussein's first Scud missile fell on the city. Welcome to Israel.

We pulled up outside Bar Doxa, and met Elan's girlfriend, Sonya, inside the bar that out-trendied anything in London, but which was devoid of metropolitan exclusivity.

A DJ played hip-hop music, but not so loud that you couldn't talk, and there was the expectation of an evening

Bauhaus: a German school of architecture
Rabin: Israeli prime minister, assassinated at a peace rally in 1995

ahead. It was 12.30 a.m. 'A Russian set up this bar,' said Elan, 'She's from Georgia. This bar – it's a good one, a lovely one.' She owned another restaurant round the corner.

He began to explain the Russian problem a little less emotionally than my cab driver. One million Russians, he said, have come to Israel in the past seven years. The population is six million. That is a significant change to the dynamic of the country, but that is what the country is like – new blood is always arriving, for better or worse. Welcome to Israel.

The bar seemed to **nurture** conversation but, after a few beers, it was time to go clubbing. At 1.30 a.m., Elan shepherded us to Ku Millennium on Salome St. Now, this showed a city that really knew how to party. A clubbing crowd danced to a heavy house sound in a space that had places where you could retreat from the music yet still be involved. And it had the most spectacular interior design. Two hundred bare lightbulbs suspended from the ceiling at different heights were raised and lowered and flashed in random sequence. Every 10 minutes or so, orange fluorescent tubes grew from recesses in the ceiling like stalactites, casting a glow across the space. This was a club, like its clubbers and city, with visual flair and **panache**.

We left at 4.30 a.m. and crashed out in the warm morning air at Humous Ashkara – an Arabic fast-food joint that sold humous by the bowlful. And this was no

nurture: encourage
panache: stylish self-confidence

ordinary humous. It was like cream filling your mouth but with an explosive garlic kick-back. A truly good and lovely one, we all agreed.

I had been in Tel Aviv for barely six hours. Already it had the better of me. I resolved to reverse the situation the next day.

As an antidote to the city and all the bright lights of the night before, I decided to spend the next morning in Jaffa, just south of Tel Aviv and only 20–30 minutes' walk away. As well as being the picturesque biblical port where Jonah stepped out of the whale, Jaffa has also been the gateway for Israel's immigrants and until 1948 had an Arab majority.

It also plays host to a flea market. Flea markets are odd, and Jaffa's is particularly so. Whatever made these stall-holders think punters would want to buy soiled sheets, tennis balls that had lost their bounce or old and clearly second-hand porn mags? But it proves the power of the market – because if such things are on sale, then someone must be buying. In among the old porn and Tom Jones in Jerusalem LPs were some great things, though: beautifully shaped cut-glass from old chandeliers, rugs, carpets and strings of amber beads at very cheap prices – all to be haggled over, of course.

The overdose of junk made me hungry and a lucky wrong turn down a side-street led to an Arab café, called Abu Hassan. In the same family for two generations, it worked on the principle of cooking up a big bean dish, called Fuul, and shutting when it had sold out.

There was a party atmosphere in the tight, little concrete building with its 50s formica tables and chairs, glasses clinking, shouting from the kitchen, even some singing. And the food was cheap: 14 shekels (£2) for a dish and a drink. I was ready to take on Tel Aviv again.

I made for Sheinken Street, the **epicentre** of fashionable Tel Aviv. It was 4 p.m. and things were hotting up. The really chic poseurs were carrying little puppies around in their arms or sitting with them at café tables. Those who didn't yet have this week's model could buy then from one of the couple of puppy vendors on the street.

But the real sign of Israeli Tel Aviv chic was an M16 machine gun. Not for sale on the street or in the shops, but sexy national service girls and boys dressed in combat fatigues with Ray-Bans slung their weapons over their shoulders or propped them against the café table while chatting, laughing and drinking. I wasn't sure how safe it made me feel, so I made for the beach to watch the sun go down.

Hundreds of others had the same idea, and many brought bongos to play. They danced on the sand, limbering up for the evening. I rang Elan on his mobile.

'Meet me at the Club Barbie on Salome Street,' he said. 'You'll like it … '
'It's a good and lovely one?' I ventured 'Yes.'

Club Barbie is the kind of place you would expect to see the Velvet Underground play – a warehouse space with makeshift décor giving the feeling of a bomb shelter with a 60s atmosphere. There's a big open courtyard too, which was great to sit out

epicentre: hub

in under the warm Tel Aviv sky. I told Elan about the M16s and he laughed. He had done his bit in the army, like all Israelis, and he had done it at a bad time – during the Lebanon.

He then recalled Tel Aviv during the Gulf War – the fear of Scud attacks and the intensity of life lived under bombing. It seemed a long way from where we were now. As we were talking, a friend of his, Jossie, came over. He had lived in New York for many years but had recently returned to Tel Aviv. With Rudi Giuliani's reforms, he said, New York had lost the edge that Tel Aviv still has – and it was always sunny and hot here. This city has a special buzz, he said.

Jossie was right. Tel Aviv has the edge of Belfast, the spirit of Rio, where parties start on the beach, and the 24-hour attitude of a big city – with plenty of art, theatre and music, too, if you want it.

On my last morning, I took a quick spin around Tel Aviv's art gallery, which houses Chagall, Picasso and even Hogarth, and then took a taxi to the airport. The cab went along the coast road and I looked at the seafront's high-rise hotels mixing with the minarets of a mosque. This place really is a collision of many things.

I asked the taxi driver how long had he lived in Tel Aviv, how much had it changed since he had been here. He looked at me blankly and said 'I don't speak English – I'm Russian.'

A holiday brochure perspective on the French capital

from Cresta Holidays brochure

Paris! City of romance, great food and wine! (And also the Eiffel Tower, Notre Dame, the Louvre and the River Seine.)

Another travel company tries to make us spend our money on a trip to the French capital (with them of course!).

Paris is the most accessible of Europe's great cities – more compact, arguably more stylish and considerably cheaper than London. Competition between travel companies selling 'short break' holidays in the French capital is therefore fierce. How easily would the Cresta Holidays brochure persuade *you* to book your ticket?

Paris

… the very name conjures up a multitude of images. Pavement artists in Montmartre's lively Place du Tertre; evening cruises down the majestic Seine under the famous bridges, past illuminated buildings of fairytale enchantment; the cool, dark solemnity and brilliant splashes of colour in Notre Dame Cathedral; dusty bookstalls along the Left Bank and Bohemian restaurants in the Latin Quarter. And you still haven't begun to describe this wonderful city!
Spend time exploring the secrets of the Louvre, stroll along the Rive Gauche and sip an aperitif at the Deux

Magots in St Germain whilst enjoying the antics of fire eaters, musicians and clowns in the cobbled square. Promenade down the Champs Elysées at dusk or take in a razzle dazzle cabaret show at the Moulin Rouge, just one of many superb cabarets in town.

Whatever your style and whatever your budget, Paris has something to suit everyone. From the simplest delights to the most elaborate spectacles, this city will delight you time and again!

Sights Our Travel Pack includes our superb guide book, a street map, Métro plan and other handy hints on getting around Paris, but we suggest you book an optional guided tour as a good way to get your bearings. Apart from the major sights we also suggest the Orangerie Gallery in the Tuileries Gardens, with its Impressionist art including Monet's fabulous Water Lilies; the Latin Quarter in the streets around St Severin off the boulevard St Michel; promenades along the Seine between Pont de la Concorde and Notre Dame including the two islands; the Tuileries Gardens where children sail boats in the round ponds; the Bois de Boulogne with its lakes, cafés and walled garden, Parc de Bagatelle. Many museums close Tuesday and French bank holidays, but admission is often half price or free on Sunday. Finally, for the best views of the city ascend the Eiffel Tower, Sacré Coeur's steps or the Montparnasse Tower.

Relaxing Paris is once again no more expensive than London and sometimes cheaper. Even on the famous Champs Elysées you can buy a 2 course meal for around FF75. Look out for the 'Plat du Jour' and 'Menu Prix Fixe' chalked on blackboards and try the small restaurants of St Germain, Montmartre or the boulevard du Montparnasse. Pavement cafes are favourite places for people-watching – the Café de la Paix in the Grand Hotel by the Opéra is one of the most famous. If you want to splash out then Le Doyen on the Champs Elysées or La Tour d'Argent overlooking Notre Dame are superb. For a special occasion, take in one of the famous cabaret shows which can be pre-booked through Cresta.

Shops Department stores like Galéries Lafayette and Le Printemps open Mon–Sat 0930-1830. Smaller shops often close Monday. The top boutiques are in rue du Faubourg St Honoré, at Les Halles and in St Germain. At the other end of the scale try flea markets like Marché aux Puces at Porte de Clignancourt (Sat, Sun & Mon) and Place d'Aligré (mornings except Mon) or colourful Rue Mouffetard behind the Pantheon and the Sunday bird market at Place Louis-Lepine. The most famous food store in Paris is Fauchon at Place de la Madeleine, but for good value try the Monoprix supermarkets.

Problems in Paris
from Neither Here nor There
by Bill Bryson

Bill Bryson is far less convinced of the joys of the French capital . . .

On my first trip to Paris I kept wondering, Why does everyone hate me so much? Fresh off the train, I went to the tourist booth at the **Gare du Nord**, where a severe young woman in a blue uniform looked at me as if I were infectious. 'What do *you* want?' she said, or at least seemed to say.

'I'd like a room, please,' I replied, instantly meek.

'Fill this out.' She pushed a long form at me. 'Not here. Over there.' She indicated with a flick of her head a counter for filling out forms, then turned to the next person in line and said 'What do *you* want?' I was amazed – I came from a place where *everyone* was friendly, where even funeral directors told you to have a nice day as you left to bury your grandmother – but I soon learned that everyone in Paris was like that. You would go into a bakery and be greeted by some vast slug-like creature with a look that told you you would never be friends. In halting French you would ask for a small loaf of bread. The woman would give you a long, cold stare and then put a dead beaver on the counter.

'No, no,' you would say, hands aflutter, 'not a dead beaver. A loaf of *bread*.'

The slug-like creature would stare at you in patent disbelief, then turn to the other customers and address

---

Gare du Nord: a railway station in Paris

them in French at much too high speed for you to follow, but the drift of which clearly was that this person here, this *American tourist*, had come in and asked for a dead beaver and she had given him a dead beaver and now he was saying that he didn't want a dead beaver at all, he wanted a loaf of bread. The other customers would look at you as if you had just tried to fart in their handbags, and you would have no choice but to slink away and console yourself with the thought that in another four days you would be in Brussels and probably able to eat again.

Activities

The origins of Australia's greatest city

1 Imagine that you are writing a guidebook on Sydney.
Using the information in the extract, make a list on aspects
of Sydney that might be of interest to visitors. Use the
following headings:

- Landmarks
- Activities
- Places to go
- Monuments
- Local transport
- Weather

2 Give examples of how the writer makes the description of
Sydney vivid for the reader by:

- using local slang words and expressions
- dropping in 'snippets' of historical information
- sharing 'local' knowledge.

3 Re-read paragraphs 1 and 2 on page 82.

How does the writer create the harbour scene? Copy the
grid below and write as many examples as you can find
for each heading in the right-hand box:

Subject	Adjectives
yachts ferry boats	slithery, majestic
	Verbs
yachts ferry boats pleasure craft	skim, loiter
	Similes
racing yachts	like thunderbolts

4 Now look at question 1 on page 117.

From Here to There

Kiev and the KGB

1 The events described in this extract take place in the Russian city of Kiev, but we learn little about the city itself. Why do you think this is?

Brainstorm words that describe the atmosphere created in this extract.

brooding   menace   watchful

2 The writer uses very particular and often quite unusual words to make his meaning clear. Use a dictionary or a thesaurus and write down one alternative word (or short phrase) meaning the same as each of the following:

- vigilance
- scrutinised
- inquisition
- fastidiously

3 Make a list of the ways in which Colin Thubron feels he is being watched by the KGB. The list has been started for you.

Telephone enquiries to hotel staff
Following his car when he goes out

4 Imagine that you are a member of the KGB (the Russian secret police) assigned to follow Colin Thubron and report on his movements. Write a report on the methods you used to monitor his activities, based on the information in the extract.

Remember that in a report, the writing should be:

- linear (all the events should be written down in the correct order)
- formal (using precise and unemotional language)
- clear and accurate.

4 Now look at question 1 on page 117.

London parks

1 What does this guide assume will interest most visitors to the parts of London described in this extract?

2 Who do you think would buy and use this type of guidebook? Give reasons for your answer.

3 Which of the following statements can correctly be applied to this extract? Write down each statement you judge to be true, and give an example from the text.

- The extract offers advice on places of interest.
- The extract seeks to persuade people to visit places of interest.
- The descriptions are fair and impartial.
- The descriptions are designed to 'sell' the location.
- Adjectives are used to give an exaggerated impression.
- Adjectives are used to give an accurate impression.
- Detailed and accurate information is given.
- The information given is general and not detailed.

4 As a class, discuss what visitors would find interesting about your own town (or the nearest town). Brainstorm a list of your town's principal attractions for a visitor.

Divide into small groups, each with a brief to research one of the headings below. Between them, the groups should cover as many of the headings as possible.

- Location
- Trade and Industry
- Theatres, Cinemas and Concert Halls
- Museums and Libraries
- Local Crafts and Produce
- Where to Eat Out
- Places to see
- Shopping
- Events
- Sport
- Nightlife
- History

Each group, under its chosen heading, should write a section of a guide book. All groups should use a style similar to that employed in the extract, to provide maximum information with minimum 'hard sell'.

5 Now look at question 1 on page 117.

Nightlife in Beirut and 48 Hours in Tel Aviv

1 Copy the table below and list the advantages and disadvantages of living in each city. If you had to live in one of the two cities, which would you prefer?

Beirut		Tel Aviv	
Advantages	*Disadvantages*	*Advantages*	*Disadvantages*

Nightlife in Beirut

2 a Find three examples of humorous statements that make light of the horrors of war-torn Beirut.
  b Find three examples of serious advice for survival in the city.

What are the differences in tone and style between the humorous and serious pieces you have selected?

3 Did P.J. O'Rourke enjoy his stay in Beirut, or did he hate it? Was he excited or terrified?

Is it possible to tell from the extract what the author's feelings were? Why/why not?

48 Hours in Tel Aviv

4 a The writer uses the words 'it's a good one, it's a lovely one' several times in the course of his article. How does the repetition affect the atmosphere of the extract?
  b The expression 'Welcome to Israel' is used twice. Why does the writer use it at these points? Try reading the extract without 'Welcome to Israel'. What is lost by leaving it out?

5 Now look at question 1 on page 117.

A holiday brochure perspective on the French capital and Problems in Paris

A holiday brochure perspective on the French capital

1 The first paragraph of the introduction to this extract is full of adjectives. Some of these are single words (e.g. famous), others are phrases that are used as adjectives (e.g. 'of fairytale enchantment').

   a Write out the first paragraph of the introduction from '. . . the very name conjures up a multitude of images' to 'to describe this wonderful city'. Write all the adjectives in capital letters.

   b There aren't as many adjectives in the second paragraph. Write down the following extract from this paragraph and fill each of the blanks with a suitable adjectives. The first one has been done for you.

Spend time exploring the _fascinating_ secrets of the Louvre, stroll along the _____ River Gauche and sip an aperitif at the _____ Deux Magots in St Germain whilst enjoying the _____ antics of fire eaters, musicians and clowns in the _____ cobbled square . . . .

Problems in Paris

2 Which statement below do you agree with? Why?

   a The writer is giving a true account of an actual experience.

   b The writer is giving an exaggerated account of the sort of experience a traveller in Paris might expect to have.

3 The writer does not seem to share the view of Paris and its people given in the holiday brochure. Write down three examples of adjectives – e.g. *severe* (page 109) or phrases that are used as adjectives – e.g. 'as if I was infectious' (page 109) that help give the impression of what he feels.

4 Choose a famous or interesting place or feature that you have visited, such as a building, public place, monument or landscape.

  a Write a holiday brochure-style description of it in glowing terms, to convince a tourist that it is a 'must see' attraction.

  b Design a poster, leaflet or web page featuring your chosen attraction.

5 Collect holiday brochures, particularly ones featuring places you have actually been to.

- How closely do the promises of the brochures match the reality?
- Should holiday companies be allowed to make exaggerated claims, or do people see through these anyway?
- Would you prefer a more informative (and possible honest) style of brochure, or do you think travel brochures are fine as they are?

6 Now look at question 1 on page 117.

Comparing texts

1 Each piece of travel writing has a particular purpose. The **language** and **structure** of a piece of writing helps get this purpose across to the reader. For each extract in this section use a format like the one on page 194 (see a completed example on page 196) to write a report on how these pieces of travel writing achieve their effect.

2 Which of the cities described in this section would you most like to visit? Why?

Which of the cities described in this section would you least like to visit? Why?

3 Which of these extracts are mainly concerned with giving facts, and which with giving opinions? Copy and complete the grid below:

Extracts giving facts	Extracts giving opinions	Extracts giving both
London parks	Problems in Paris	Nightlife in Beirut

4 Choose one extract from the section which is mostly concerned with describing a place and one which is mostly concerned with describing people. Use the reports you have completed to comment on the **text type**, **language**, **tone**, **narrator**, **address** and **period** of each extract, to show how each writer uses a different style to achieve his or her purpose.

5 Choose one of the following extracts and rewrite it in the style suggested. Make sure you use the features that you have identified as belonging to that style.

Extract	Rewrite in the style of
London parks (pages 91–95) (Write on any sub-headings)	→ **A holiday brochure perspective on the French capital** (pages 106–108)
The origins of Australia's → **greatest city** from 'Of course, everyone had long . . .' (page 83) to '. . . they nearly always won' (page 84) your *or* **Nightlife in Beirut** → The first two paragraphs (pages 96–97)	Write a hard-sell holiday brochure on the delights of chosen city – London, Sydney or Beirut

6 Choose one of the styles you have studied in this section to write about a city that you have visited, or that you have read about or researched. Remember to include the features that you have identified for that style, and to:

- decide whether you will need to report facts or give opinions

- decide whether you are interested mostly in the place or its people.

Whichever style you choose, you will need to use adjectives, verbs and similes to make your account as vivid and interesting as possible for the reader. Your descriptions will need to be very full and clear, as your readers may never have visited the city you have chosen to write about.

Section 4
Roots

Another reason for travelling is to discover where people have come from. Some travellers (like Tahir Shah and V. S. Naipaul) are trying to find their own roots by returning to the countries of their ancestors. Others (like Laurens van der Post and Tim Severin) are more interested in the origins of other peoples, and the epic journeys they made in order to find new lands and new homes – or the journeys that others started but never finished ...

The Search for Mallory and Irvine
from Ghosts of Everest
by Jochen Hemmleb, Larry A. Johnson,
and Eric R. Simonson

On 6 June 1924, two British climbers, George Mallory and Andrew Irvine, set off from their camp high on the North Face of Mount Everest. Their aim was to become the first men to reach the summit of the mountain.

George Mallory was the greatest climber of the time. When he was asked why he wanted to climb Everest he replied, 'Because it's there!'.

As Mallory and Irvine climbed towards the highest spot on Earth, they were seen by another climber, Noel

Odell, at 12.50. Odell claimed that they were 800 feet below the summit. Then they disappeared. They were never seen alive again.

The fate of Mallory and Irvine became the greatest mystery of the mountain. What had happened to them? Had they succeeded in reaching the summit of Everest?

In 1979, a Chinese climber called Wang Hongbao told a Japanese climber that he had found an 'English dead' – the body of an English climber – on an earlier Everest expedition. Although he didn't speak any Japanese, Wang managed to explain where he had found the body. However, the next day he was killed by an avalanche.

In 1999, the Mallory and Irvine Research Expedition team set off to follow the steps of the 1924 expedition. From Wang's account, and other evidence, they had concluded that Wang had found the body of Andrew Irvine. They expected a long and difficult search. Incredibly, only a few hours after reaching the search area, the team made an astounding discovery.

Conrad Anker had been going on intuition, and his intuition had told him to look low. He had climbed down to the lower edge of the terrace, the point where it dropped away some 6,600 feet (2,000 m) to the main Rongbuk Glacier, and had started zigzagging back up the slope when he saw 'a patch of white that was whiter than the rock around it and whiter than the snow'. Climbing toward it, he realised the patch of white was another body. But this one was different: ' . . . this wasn't a body from recent times; it was something that had been there for quite a while.'

Norton was the first to reach Anker. 'I'm afraid I wasn't very eloquent,' he recalls. 'I just sat down on a rock next to Conrad, looked at this perfect alabaster body, and said to myself, "Holy shit!" I had harboured no hope that we'd find anything this first day. We just expected to do a reconnaissance of the area. It was just amazing.'

As Dave Hahn approached the site and saw the body, he recalls: 'There was absolutely no question in my mind that we were looking at a man who had been clinging to the mountain for seventy-five years. The clothing was blasted from most of his body and his skin was bleached white. I felt like I was viewing a Greek or Roman marble statue.'

There was no exultation when the climbers all reached the site, no 'high fives' signalling that, only an hour and a half into a search of a vast section of the North Face of Mount Everest, they had found their man. Instead, the five modern climbers stood or kneeled around the ancient body, speechless.

The body itself did the speaking. For here was a body unlike the others crumpled in crannies elsewhere on the terrace. This body was lying fully extended, face down and pointing uphill, frozen in a position of self-arrest, as

if the fall had happened only moments earlier. The head and upper torso were frozen into the rubble that had gathered around them over the decades, but the arms, powerfully muscular still, extended above the head to strong hands that gripped the mountainside, flexed fingertips dug deep into the frozen gravel. The legs were extended downhill. One was broken and the other had been gently crossed over it for protection. Here too, the musculature was still pronounced and powerful. The entire body had about it the strength and grace of a dancer. This body, this man, had once been a splendid specimen of humankind.

'We weren't just looking at a body,' Hahn explains, 'we were looking at an era, one we'd only known through books. The natural-fibre clothes, the fur-lined leather helmet, the kind of rope that was around him were all so eloquent. As we stood there, this mute but strangely peaceful body was telling us answers to questions that everyone had wondered about for three-quarters of a century: the fact that a rope had been involved; the fact that the hands and forearms were much darker than the rest of the body; the nature and extent of the broken leg and what wasn't broken, and what that said about this person's last moments; the fact that there was no oxygen apparatus.'

The hobnail boot, of course, was the giveaway. No westerner was permitted on Everest from 1949 until 1979; Tibet, the 'Forbidden Kingdom', was forbidden to outsiders. No one had died at this altitude on Everest between 1924 and 1938, and hobnailed boots had given way to crampons and more advanced boot construction by World War II. The body had to be Andrew Comyn Irvine. Jake Norton went so far as to begin scratching out a memorial stone with the words, 'Andrew Irvine: 1902–1924.'

'This isn't him,' Andy Politz said to the rest of the climbers when he arrived at the spot where the others waited.

The rest of the team looked at Politz as if he were daft. 'Oh, I think so,' Anker said.

'I don't know what made me say it,' Politz now says. 'Here was this very old body, perfectly preserved, with very old clothing and the hobnailed boots. I knew it had to be Irvine; Irvine was who we were looking for, and that's who it had to be.'

But it wasn't.

Tap Richards, who had training in Archeology, and Jake Norton began gently separating the ragged layers of clothing that were left around the protected edges of the body: several layers of cotton and silk underwear, a flannel shirt, woollen pullover and trousers, a canvaslike outer garment. Near the nape of the neck, Norton turned over a piece of shirt collar and revealed a fragment of laundry label: *G. Mallory*.

The climbers looked at each other dumbly for a moment, and finally someone said out loud what everyone else was thinking: 'Why would Irvine be wearing Mallory's shirt?' Then they found another name tag: *G. Leigh Ma[llory]*. Then a third.

'Maybe it was the altitude and the fact that we'd all put aside our oxygen gear, but it took a while for reality to sink in,' says Hahn. 'Then it finally hit us: we had not found Andrew Irvine. We had not rediscovered Wang Hongbao's "English dead". We were in the presence of George Mallory himself . . . the man whose boldness and drive we'd grown up in awe of.'

'Now I realised why I had said it wasn't Irvine,' Politz explained later. 'It was the position of the body. Somewhere back in my subconscious, my intuition remembered that Wang had found a body that had been in a position where his mouth was agape and his cheek was exposed to the **goraks**. But this body was face down.

---

goraks: mountain ravens living on the slopes of Everest

The head was almost entirely covered, and it had not been moved. What's more, it was too far from the 1975 Chinese **Camp VI** to have ever been found on a short walk. I just sat down. My knees literally got weak. My jaw dropped. Next to me, Dave was saying, "Oh my God, it's George. Oh my God."'

It had been an article of faith that if anyone had fallen, it would have been the inexperienced Andrew Irvine. 'Throughout the seventy-five years since they disappeared,' explains Jake Norton, 'it had been understood that George Mallory was infallible, he didn't fall, he couldn't fall. It was a shock to discover that he was fallible, he did fall. We couldn't quite get used to the idea.'

Meanwhile, however, time was passing. The climbers had a responsibility to document as professionally as possible what they had found, search for artifacts, provide Mallory a proper burial, and perform a Church of England committal service provided by the Anglican Bishop of Bristol, England. After that, they still had a two- to-three hour descent to Camp V to negotiate safely. 'It would have been nice to have been able to leave the work for another day,' says Hahn, 'but on Everest, there are no guaranteed second chances; the **monsoon** could start tomorrow.'

There was another issue as well: 'We knew we were going to have to disturb him to do our job,' Hahn explains, 'and we only wanted to disturb him once. Then we wanted to leave him in peace. We knew if we did not do a thorough search for the camera and other artifacts, people would keep coming back and disturbing him again.'

The first thing the climbers had done when they discovered the body – before they touched it, before they discovered who it was – was to document photographically both the site and the body. Then they

---

Camp VI: the highest camp established by the Chinese expedition
monsoon: season of maximum rain- or snowfall in India and Pakistan

discussed what to do next. 'It came down to trying to decide what Mallory himself would have wanted,' explains Politz. 'In the end, Dave put it best: "If we can find some evidence of what he accomplished, especially whether he and Irvine had made it to the summit, I think he'd want the world to know."' As they stood around this man, this icon of Everest itself, the others agreed, and it was time to go to work.

Their main objective, of course, was to find the famous camera, the collapsible Kodak Vestpocket camera that Howard Somervell had lent Mallory for the summit attempt – the mechanism that would answer, it was hoped, the question of whether Mount Everest had been summited in 1924, more than a quarter century before Edmund Hillary and Tenzing Norgay did it by another route in 1953. In the cold, dry air of the mountain, Kodak officials had said, there was every reason to believe the film, if intact, would still be able to be developed.

The camera was not beside George Mallory's body and it seemed reasonable to assume that, if he had it, it would be in a pocket or around his neck – neither of which were immediately accessible, as Mallory was effectively locked in the icy embrace of the North Face.

The task before them was formidable. 'It was immediately apparent,' Hahn says, 'that this was going to be neither simple, easy, or quick.' Politz elaborates, 'If you took a one-pound ice axe and started chopping concrete with it, you'd get the same effect as what it was like to try to chip away at the frozen gravel and rock that encased roughly half of George Mallory on the slope,' Politz explains. 'It was just brutally hard work.'

It was also dangerous. The ground was uneven and very steeply sloped and, says Hahn, 'a single misstep could easily send you down the slope and over the edge. When you got up off your knees, you wanted to be very sure where your feet were going to be. To keep things interesting, every once in a while a rock would go whizzing past our heads.'

As they worked on the ice, the climbers could not get used to how little Mallory had been wearing during his attempt to reach the highest point on earth. 'We're standing there in down suits so thick that I couldn't even see the climbing harness around my waist,' Hahn explains. 'In our packs we had food, water, electronic gear, and extra mittens, and here was this man before us who was wearing what maybe added up to the equivalent of two layers of fleece. Hell, I walk out on the street in Seattle with more clothing than he had on at 28,000 feet on Everest! Clearly they were tough climbers, but there wasn't any room for anything to go wrong for these guys, no margin at all.'

The five members of the Mallory and Irvine Research Expedition recovered many items of interest from Mallory's body before piling rocks over it – the nearest they could manage to a proper burial. What they found gave a lot more information about the fate of Mallory and Irvine.

Although the expedition succeeded in putting two climbers on the summit of Everest, they did not find the camera, and they did not find Irvine's body. The most vital question – did Mallory and Irvine reach the summit? – may never be answered.

Skylla and Charybdis
from The Odyssey
by Homer

Homer was the greatest poet of the Ancient Greeks. Two epic poems about the Trojan War are all that survive of his work. In *The Iliad*, he describes the ten-year siege and destruction of the great city of Troy by the Greeks.

In *The Odyssey*, Homer tells the story of a Greek general called Odysseus and his journey home from Troy to Greece, which took over ten years! Odysseus and his men are blown across the Mediterranean Sea by storms created by angry Greek gods. During the journey Odysseus has many adventures, most of which are dangerous!

In this extract, Odysseus and his men have just escaped from the spell of the Sirens (whose voices make men throw themselves to their deaths in the sea). Unfortunately, it is a case of 'out of the frying pan and into the fire'. Odysseus and his men are about to face two more terrors: the monster Scylla (spelt Skylla here) and the whirlpool, Charybdis.

. . . the next thing
we saw was smoke, and a heavy surf, and we heard it thundering.
The men were terrified, and they let the oars fall out of
their hands, and these banged all about in the wash. The ship stopped
still, with the men no longer rowing to keep way on her.
Then I going up and down the ship urged on my companions,
standing beside each man and speaking to him in kind words:

'Dear friends, surely we are not unlearned in evils.
This is no greater evil now than it was when the **Cyclops**
had us cooped in his hollow cave by force and violence,
but even there, by my courage and counsel and my intelligence,
we escaped away. I think that all this will be remembered
some day too. Then do as I say, let us all be won over.
Sit well, all of you, to your oarlocks, and dash your oars deep
into the breaking surf of the water, so in that way Zeus
might grant that we get clear of this danger and flee away from it.
For you, steersman, I have this order; so store it deeply
in your mind, as you control the steering oar of this hollow
ship; you must keep her clear from where the smoke and the breakers
are, and make hard for the sea rock lest, without your knowing,
she might drift that way, and you bring all of us into disaster.'

'So I spoke, and they quickly obeyed my words. I had not
spoken yet of Skylla, a plague that could not be dealt with,
for fear my companions might be terrified and give over
their rowing, and take cover inside the ship. For my part,
I let go from my mind the difficult instruction that **Circe**
had given me, for she told me not to be armed for combat;
but I put on my glorious armour and, taking up two long
spears in my hands, I stood bestriding the vessel's foredeck
at the prow, for I expected Skylla of the rocks to appear first
from that direction, she who brought pain to my companions.
I could not make her out anywhere, and my eyes grew weary
from looking everywhere on the misty face of the sea rock.

'So we sailed up the narrow strait lamenting. On one side
was Skylla, and on the other side was shining Charybdis,
who made her terrible ebb and flow of the sea's water.
When she vomited it up, like a cauldron over a strong fire,
the whole sea would boil up in turbulence, and the foam flying
spattered the pinnacles of the rocks in either direction;
but when in turn again she sucked down the sea's salt water,
the turbulence showed all the inner sea, and the rock around it
groaned terribly, and the ground showed at the sea's bottom,

Cyclops: a man-eating, one-eyed giant called Polyphemus, who imprisoned Odysseus' crew in his cave.

Circe: a goddess who protected Odysseus. She told him not to fight Skylla, who had six heads, each big enough to swallow a man.

black with sand; and green fear seized upon my companions.
We in fear of destruction kept our eyes on Charybdis,
but meanwhile Skylla out of the hollow vessel snatched six
of my companions, the best of them for strength and hands' work,
and when I turned to look at the ship, with my other companions,
I saw their feet and hands from below, already lifted
high above me, and they cried out to me and called me
by name, the last time they ever did it, in heart's sorrow.
And as a fisherman with a very long rod, on a jutting
rock, will cast his treacherous bait for the little fishes,
and sinks the horn of a field-ranging ox into the water,
then hauls them up and throws them on the dry land, gasping
and struggling, so they gasped and struggled as they were hoisted
up the cliff. Right in her doorway she ate them up. They were screaming
and reaching out their hands to me in this horrid encounter.
That was the most pitiful scene that these eyes have looked on
in my sufferings as I explored the routes over the water.

In search of Scylla's Cave
from The Ulysses Voyage
by Tim Severin

In 1985, Tim Severin and his crew tried to retrace Odysseus' journey from Troy. In a reconstructed Greek galley ship called the Argo, he set off to try to discover the truth about the many legends surrounding Homer's hero. His search for the location of Scylla's Cave led him to the island of Levkas in the Cyclades ...

I was so confident that we were on the brink of solving the riddle of the narrow straits of Scylla and Charybdis on Ulysses' journey that I went ashore to search for Scylla's Cave feeling that it would be there. I had compared the description of the cave in the *Odyssey* with the large-scale chart and knew just where to start looking. The rock in whose side Scylla dwelt, Circe said, 'rears its sharp peak up to the very sky and is capped by black clouds that never stream away nor leave clear weather round the top, even in summer or in harvest time'.

Of course Homer was exaggerating the lofty peak with its perpetual cloud. Nevertheless there was the peak of Mount Lamia standing above the bay, and the usual west wind blowing in from the sea struck the summit and left a trail of **orographic** cloud streaming from its crest in an otherwise clear sky. Scylla's cave had to be in the flank of Mount **Lamia**, the Mountain of the Long-Necked Devouring Monster. The directions within the legend were there in front of me; I had only to apply them to the

---

orographic: relating to mountains
Lamia: a dragon-like monster: possibly another name for Scylla

physical reality, reading the poet's word pictures as a description of the countryside.

The flank of Mount Lamia was steep but not as unclimbable as Homer would have us believe: 'no man on earth could climb it, up or down, not even with twenty hands and feet to help him; for the rock is as smooth as if it had been polished.'

The steepest section of Mount Lamia's flank was close above the modern road, a promising-looking crag of near-vertical cliff. The gentler lower slope was covered with bushes growing in the **detritus** that had slumped down the hillside. The crag itself was in exactly the right position, for it faced west over the bay where *Argo* had anchored behind Plaka Spit, and Circe had told Ulysses that 'halfway up the crag is a misty cavern, facing the West and running down to Erebus, past which, my lord Odysseus, you must steer your ship'.

Erebus was the land of the departed spirits, to the west, and Scylla's cave had to be fairly high up, for Circe continued that 'the strongest bowman could not reach the gaping mouth of the cave with an arrow shot from a ship below'.

Two men were in a punt below me as I walked along the road between Canali Stretti and the section of cliff. They were poised with immensely long-handled fish tridents and stared intently at the water, fishing for eels in the shallows of the waterway. 'The cave!' I shouted down to them. 'Where's the cave?' They looked up, startled. I realised that I was so sure that I would find the cave that I hadn't even asked, 'Is there any cave near here?' or some such general question. 'The cave? Where?' I yelled again. The fishermen were clearly annoyed to be disturbed. They turned their backs. I persisted. 'The cave! Please, the cave?' hoping that my very clumsy Greek

---

detritus: mass of rock fragments

pronunciation would be understood. The cave had to be nearby. I saw the two men confer, witnessed an irritated shrug. Obviously they thought I was a crazy tourist, and I caught the word 'Antonis' [Anthony]. Then in final exasperation before he turned back to his eel-spearing, one of the men gestured at the cliff behind me. Turning, I could just make out the corner of some sort of balcony with an iron railing projecting beyond the branches of an ancient olive tree, high up the crag. With growing excitement I hurried down the tarmac road until I found a footpath leading up the hillside. The path zigzagged back and forth, and hadn't been used recently for I pushed through cobwebs spun between the bushes. The fat spiders reminded me of Scylla, sitting in her lair waiting to seize the passing victims, for I *knew* that I was on the right track.

The path brought me to a short flight of steps, and these led me up on to the concrete balcony which I had noticed earlier. The balcony was something to do with a church, for there was a crude cross made of two extra pieces of the metal rail welded together, and a large bell was hung on a frame of metal pipes. A tiled roof had been built out from the cliff face as a sort of porch, and at the back of the balcony were two small windows and a brown painted door led into the cliff face. On closer inspection I saw that the door was set in a section of man-made wall which had been constructed to fill in the overhang of rock. Above the door was a large iron key on a nail. I unlocked the door and, feeling like Alice walking through the looking glass, stepped inside.

I was standing in a cave. It had been turned into a chapel, but the shape and atmosphere of the original grotto were not masked in any way. Its walls were grotesque. They were blobbed and runnelled like melted wax and streaked with smoke from the offertory candles. The highest point of the cave was about fifteen feet and it was some twelve feet deep and about thirty feet wide, a gloomy hole scooped in the cliff face. It was the perfect den for Scylla.

I turned and walked back on to the balcony, with my back to the cave mouth. Circe's directions fitted perfectly. Below me I could distinguish the line of the ancient channel where it wound close against the foot of the cliff.

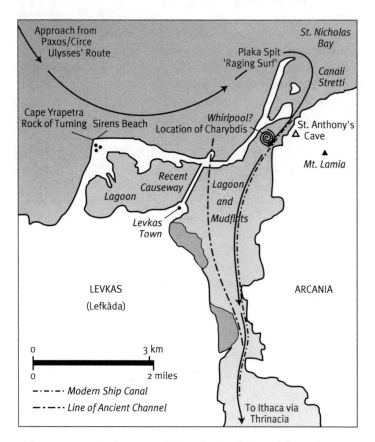

Map showing the location of the whirlpool Charybdis and St. Anthony's cave where Scylla preyed on Odysseus' crew

From my vantage point I could look down like an osprey and see the wriggling patterns of small eels disturbing the fine pale yellow mud of the shallows of Canali Stretti. Directly ahead was the Plaka Spit with its straight line of waves still breaking in foam, though it was evening and the wind had calmed. Beyond the spit in the distance was the nose of Yrapetra Point, the place of the mysterious tumuli and the likely beach of the Sirens. I was standing just as Circe had said, in a cave, halfway up the cliff face, over the channel, and looking towards the west. Below me the eel fishermen had packed up for the day and were poling their way out of the shallows, using the ancient waterway. Scylla's Cave was found.

A brahmin picnic
from An Area of Darkness
by V. S. Naipaul

V. S. Naipaul was born and brought up in the West Indies. He moved to England when he was eighteen.

In 1960 he decided to travel around India. It was the country of his ancestors, but he had never visited it. His journey was certainly an eye-opener. He found many Indian customs and manners baffling, which placed him in some embarrassing situations.

In this extract, Naipaul 'gatecrashes' a family day out and has to share their picnic.

It was a cool day when we went to **Awantipur**, the dry fields a warm brown against the dark grey-blue mountains. We could make little of the ruins, the massive central platform, the anvil-shaped fonts of solid stone that lay among the rubble, the carvings; and the villager who attached himself to us didn't help. 'It all fell down,' he said in Hindustani, waving a hand. 'All?' 'All.' It was a type of North Indian dialogue, made possible by the stresses of the language, which I had grown to enjoy. He showed the base of a column and indicated by gestures that it was the bottom stone of a **quern**. That was the limit of his knowledge. No tip for him; and we walked down to the village to wait for a bus.

The blue-shirted boys had just been released from school; down a side lane we saw the young Sikh teacher organising a ball game in the schoolyard. The boys

Awantipur: a ruined temple

quern: an assembly of two millstones, used for grinding corn

gathered around us; they all carried enormous bundles of books wrapped in grubby, inky cloths. We made one boy take out his English book. He opened it at a page headed 'Our Pets', read out: 'Our Body', and began reeling off text which, after a search, we found on another page. And what book was this? Urdu? They become helpless with laughter: it was Pharsi, Persian, as any child could tell. The crowd had now grown. We broke out of it, saying we wanted to get back to **Srinagar**; and they all then began waving down buses for us. Many buses passed, full; then one shot past, hesitated, stopped. A Kashmiri attempted to get on but was repelled by the conductor, who made room for us.

We sat in the back among some sensationally unwashed people, their cotton dhotis brown with dirt, and many Dalda tins. The man next to me was stretched out on the seat, clearly unwell, his eyes without expression, the pestilential Indian flies undisturbed on lips and cheek; from time to time he gave a theatrical groan, to which no one in the chattering bus paid the slightest attention. We saw that we were in a bus of 'lower-income' tourists and that we were sitting with their servants.

At the ruins the bus stopped and the khaki-clad moustached driver turned and tried to persuade his passengers to go out and have a look. No one moved. The driver spoke again, and at length one elderly man, whom we had already recognised as the wit and leader of the bus, heaved himself up with a sigh and went out. He wore a black Indian jacket, and his top-knot proclaimed him a brahmin. The others followed.

From nowhere children appeared: '*Paisa, sahib, paisa.*' 'Oh', said the leader in Hindi. 'You want money? Now what does a little child like you want money for?' '*Roti, roti,*' they chanted. 'Bread, bread.' 'Bread, eh?' He was only teasing. He gave; the others gave.

Srinagar: a city in Kashmir in the far north of India

The leader climbed to the top of the stone steps and regarded the ruins with patronage. He made a witticism; he lectured. The others idled about dutifully, looking without interest where he looked.

A sixteen-year-old boy in white flannel trousers hurried over to me and said, 'This is **Pandavas**' fort.'

I said, 'This is not a fort.'

'It is Pandavas' fort.'

'No.'

He waved hesitantly towards the leader. 'He says it's Pandavas' fort.'

'You tell him no. He doesn't know what he's talking about.'

The boy looked shocked, as though I had offered him violence. He edged away from me, turned and fled to the group around the leader.

We were all back in the bus and about to start when the leader suggested food. The conductor threw open the door again and an especially grimy manservant, old and toothless, came to life. Briskly, proprietorially, he shoved the Dalda tins along the dusty floor and lifted them out on to the verge. I began to protest at the delay; the boy in white flannels looked at me in terror; and I realised that we had fallen among a family, that the bus was chartered, that we had been offered a lift out of charity. The bus again emptied. We remained helpless in our seats, while Srinagar-bound passenger buses, visibly holding spare seats, went past.

They were a brahmin family and their vegetarian food was served according to established form. No one was allowed to touch it except the dirty old servant who, at the mention of food, had been kindled into such important activity. With the very fingers that a moment

---

Pavandas: the five legendary heroes of the Hindu epic, the *Mahabharata*

before had been rolling a crinkled cigarette and had then seized the dusty Dalda tins from off the dusty bus floor, he now – using only the right hand, of course – distributed **puris** from one tin, scooped out curried potatoes from another, and from a third secured dripping fingerfuls of chutney. He was of the right caste; nothing served by the fingers of his right hand could be unclean; and the eaters ate with relish. The verge had been deserted; now, in the twinkling of an eye, the eaters were surrounded by villagers and long-haired Kashmiri dogs. The dogs kept their distance; they stood still, their tails low and alert, the field stretching out behind them to the mountains. The villagers, men and children, stood right over the squatting eaters who, like celebrities in the midst of an admiring crowd, slightly adjusted their behaviour. They ate with noisier relish; just perceptibly they raised their voices, heightened and lengthened out their laughter. The servant, busier than ever, frowned as if made impatient by his responsibilities. His lips disappeared between his toothless gums.

The leader spoke to the servant, and the servant came to where we were. Busily, like a man with little time to waste, he slapped two puris into our hands, plastered the puris with potatoes, leaked chutney on the potatoes, and withdrew, hugging his tins, leaving us with committed right hands.

A family spokesman came to the door of the bus. 'Just *taste* our food.'

We tasted. We felt the eyes of the villagers on us. We felt the eyes of the family on us. We smiled, and ate.

The leader made overtures of friendship; he sought to include us in his conversation. We smiled; and now it was the turn of the boy in white flannels to look hostile. Still, all the way into Srinagar we smiled.

---

puris: fried bread pancakes

A witch trial in Orissa
from Sorcerer's Apprentice
by Tahir Shah

Tahir Shah was born in 1966, a descendant of the Afghan warlord and statesman, Jan Fishan Khan.

When Tahir Shah was a young boy, an Indian magician visited the family home. Years later, he decided to go to India and study to become a magician himself.

On his travels he meets Bhalu, the Trickster, a young troublemaker and con-artist who becomes his guide. It is Bhalu who discovers that a nearby village is about to hold a witchcraft trial, and persuades Tahir Shah to investigate.

Surrounded on all sides by dusty ancestral fields, the community could never have housed more than fifty farmers and their families. Most of the simple mud houses were empty. Their owners had already left. Some of the buildings had begun to collapse, their walls crumbling like dry Oxo cubes. The few villagers who had stayed were **loath** to admit their community was home to a witch. After prolonged negotiations, Bhalu discovered the wattle-and-daub dwelling in which the woman, an aged widow, was held.

With great unwillingness, the self-appointed head man related the case.

The widow's children had fled the village some two months before, journeying to **Cuttack** in search of secure jobs. The old woman had always acted strangely, but only when her sons departed did she resort to actual witchcraft. For two years in a row the village's crops of jute and

---

loath: unwilling

ground nuts had failed. The widow had been seen pacing the fields at night, soliciting evil forces. A neighbour said she observed her transform into a wild dog. Someone else noticed that some seeds she had planted had actually grown in the parched soil. Another **purported** that the ancient had turned a tank of water sour merely by glancing at it. A fourth claimed she had made three eggs disappear into thin air. The remaining villagers had gathered together to decide a course of action.

Fortunately for the widow, many of her neighbours had departed the village for nearby towns. Had there been a full turn-out, the general state of mass hysteria would certainly have found her guilty without even the most simplistic of trials. In **Orissa**, a woman condemned as a witch is customarily stoned to death on the spot. Whereas a man – or even a younger woman – accused of sorcery might use it to his advantage, claiming to be a godman, a widow with magical powers is invariably considered to be a witch.

Fortunately for her, the lack of senior villagers had led to indecision. Now that the sorceress had been arrested, no one was quite sure what to do next. The hesitation proved the extraordinary force of mass hysteria. An enraged mob of amateur witch-hunters spontaneously derives solutions.

With no need for me to prompt him, Bhalu instructed the head man that we had been sent to decide the fate of the witch. The arrival of a twelve-year-old boy and a foreigner, both ready to adjudicate, must have seemed **implausible**. But surprisingly, the head man nodded once and opened the door to the communal store-room where the witch was being held.

Cuttack: (Kataka) a town about 300 km south-west of Calcutta
purported: claimed
Orissa: a region of India, in the north-east of the country

Blinded by the daylight, and cringing as if she were about to be guillotined, the widow was pulled out and thrown on the ground. Her head was shaven, her lips were caked in dried white foam, her arms were covered in **putrescent lesions**, and her torn sari was stained with blood.

The woman was as fearful of me as the head man was. She appeared not to have set eyes upon a foreigner before. Bhalu tried to explain that we had come to judge her case. We would listen to the evidence against her a point at a time.

The first witness was called.

A man in his fifties, he had spied the witch strolling in the fields beneath a full moon. She had been speaking to hidden spirits.

'Bhalu,' I said, 'please ask the widow why she was in the field at night, talking to herself.'

The Trickster translated my question and, with distinct difficulty, her reply.

'She says she had been unable to sleep. Her sons had left her all alone. She was miserable because the family's crop of jute had not grown. So she went out into the field and asked **Varuna** to bring rain.'

'There's no witchcraft in that,' I said. 'Move on to the next point. Ask her if she turned into a wild dog.'

The scam-artist enquired if the widow had indeed transformed herself into a 'werewolf'. Ducking her head to veil her face with the hem of her white sari, the woman mimed out an answer.

'Bhalu, can you understand what she's saying?'

'Yes . . . she says the whole village knows the problem of wild dogs. Last year two children were killed

---

implausible: unlikely
putrescent lesions: infected sores
Varuna: god of the oceans, and bringer of rain

and eaten by the hounds. But on both occasions, she was with her neighbours in the village.'

'Ask the head man if this is true.'

Bhalu interpreted the question and, grudgingly, the chief villager nodded.

'Next point . . . tell her to take us to the place where her seeds grew.'

Bhalu helped the widow to her feet. Stumbling forward, she led us, and the frantic crowd which had gathered, to a spot at the eastern edge of the village. As her shadow fell over a row of limp green shoots, the woman pointed to the bed of cultivated soil. Curiously, the area of ground was damp. Yet the surrounding earth was cracked and dry. I was about to ask Bhalu for his opinion when he pointed to a pair of water drums at the back of a nearby hut. Without saying a word, the Trickster went over and lifted the edge of the barrel. The soil beneath it was dark with moisture.

'It's got a slow leak,' he said, calling us over. 'The ground over there's wet because of this barrel of stagnant water.'

Accepting this as a plausible explanation, the head man asked the huddle of villagers for their opinion. Most remained silent. They were obviously fuelled by jealousy: the widow had succeeded in germinating a few seeds while all the other village crops had withered.

'If she's a witch,' I said, 'why didn't she make her family's field prosper instead of this pathetic patch of waste ground?'

The villagers stared at their leader and shuffled their feet. They had hunted and caught the witch and now wanted the satisfaction of punishing her.

A man called out from the back of the group.

'What's he saying, Bhalu?'

The Trickster listened to the man's protest, which was repeated several times in a loud, heckling voice.

'He says that you can explain why the seeds grew, but he wants to know why the village water soured when the witch looked at it.'

'Take us to the tank of undrinkable water.'

The **inquisition** crossed the village in silence.

A group of young women, each with large silver bangles on their wrists, were taking it in turns digging a well-shaft at the other side of the settlement. Their scant frames were, we were told, best suited to clambering down the narrow well-shaft. As the women ferried away dishes of the parched Orissan earth on their heads, we approached a large free-standing water tank next to the well.

'Is this the cistern of sour water?'

The chief villager and the heckler agreed that it was.

Bhalu removed the heap of chipped bricks holding down the water tank's cover. He signalled to three men in the mob, who helped him heave away the steel lid. As soon as I set eyes on the brackish water, I understood why it was the source of numerous afflictions. The swollen bodies of seven grey-backed bandicoot rats were floating on the surface.

At that moment a man with a club-foot hobbled over to where Bhalu, the head man and I were standing. One hand was straining to manage a crutch. In the other was an enamelled mug, filled to the brim with water. The liquid was crystal clear. The drink was as translucent as water from a mountain stream. When it was offered to him, I noticed that the Trickster refused courteously. Touched by the club-footed man's kindness, and parched with thirst, I took a long, satisfying draught.

Bhalu explained to the rabble that the rats had soured the water, not the widow's glance. The facts were all well and good, but the villagers were eager for a less scientific

---

inquisition: self-appointed court

trial. The heckler called for the old woman to be subjected to the traditional tests which would prove her guilt.

Orissa is well known for its witch trials. The procedure is usually the same. A local *Jan-guru*, a witch-hunter and amateur exorcist, is summoned. Often he starts by shaving the sorceress' head to eliminate her evil powers. Then, when the entire village has assembled, the testing begins.

Isolated from the outside world, officials find it near-impossible to regulate the trials. In any case, the authorities regard trial by ordeal as crude entertainment, and as a way for a solitary community to vent its emotions.

Before starting his elaborate inquisition, the *Jan-guru* whips up the wrath of the mob. Like hounds frenzied before a hunt, they long for the kill. The exorcist shouts the order, and the suspected witch is brought out.

Any number of tests follow. To go free the witch must pass each one. First, she may be given a *talwaar*, sword, to hold out in front of her. If the blade wavers, she's definitely a witch. Next, her mouth may be filled with dry white rice. If it's still dry when she spits it out, she's guilty. The crowd tend to overlook the fact that one's mouth is likely to dry up in the face of death.

Back in the village, the heckler was again jeering from the rear of the crowd. He was asking for the disappearing eggs to be explained.

I asked Bhalu to take a poll. If I could explain how three ordinary eggs could disappear, would they pledge a solemn oath, permitting the widow go free? The mob fell silent. At first they seemed uneasy. What if I, too, was a witch – who had come to save my fellow sorcerer? This, the unthinkable, was brushed aside. A whispered undertone rose above the hush. The head man asked his fellow villagers for their decision. Enthused at the prospect of testing me, they agreed.

Three fresh hen's eggs were brought forward by a young child. The audience gathered in an arc and watched my fingers. Some sat down, others shaded their eyes from the sun. The heckler pushed his way to the front. Beside him stood the Trickster, who wished me luck. Like the villagers he, too, fell silent. I waited for the moment. Fifty pairs of eyes gazed at me as I remembered all those hours in the Master's study. We had performed **sleights** so many times. Three eggs was a breeze for someone hardened by swallowing stones almost as large. I imagined **Hafiz Jan** peering down at me in the centre of that dusty Orissan village. 'Go on!' I seemed to hear Hafiz Jan command. 'Do it for Jan Fishan Khan!'

A pye dog hobbled from the shadows of one of the houses. It was obviously concerned why the entire village was lined up. Taking advantage of the situation, the dog **meandered** over to a child on the extreme left of the arc and sank its fangs into the infant's arm. The boy let out a piercing cry. The murderous rabble lost concentration as they turned in unison to behold the child's injuries. Seizing the moment, I flung my arms backwards and dropped the eggs down my collar. A split second later, the mob's gaze was on me again. But the eggs were nowhere to be seen.

---

sleights: conjuring tricks
Hafiz Jan: the magician who visited Tahir Shah's family when Tahir was a child, and gave him his first training in the art of magic
meandered: wandered

Encounters with Bushmen
from The Lost World of the Kalahari
by Laurens van der Post

Laurens van der Post was a white South African. He was among the first travellers to seek out the Bushmen of the Kalahari Desert (who call themselves the San or the Silent People). Here, he describes an early encounter with the San.

As we navigated our vehicles, like ships by the stars, across the sea of land I felt deeply it was not as empty of human beings as it looked. Our black servants and companions had the same feeling. Six weeks went by in which we covered some thousands of miles without meeting the Bushman. Then one evening at sundown, a hundred and fifty miles from the nearest known water, I came to a deep round pan in the central desert. It had obviously held water some weeks before and there, clearcut in the blue clay of the dried-up bottom, was a series of tiny human footprints leading up the steep sides and vanishing in the sand underneath a huge storm-tree. As I stood there in the violet light looking at the neat little casts in clay I seemed to hear the voice of the old 'Suto herder of my childhood saying again, close to my listening ear: 'His footprint, little master, is small and like no other man's and when you see it you know it at once from those of other men.'

It was clear that some weeks previously a party of authentic Bushmen had come to water at the pan. But

---

'**Suto**: man of the Sotho people, a large tribal group

though we camped there at night, and in the days that followed examined the country around, we saw no further sign of them. Sometimes, far from river, fountain or well, in the bed of steep old water-courses that have not run for centuries, we found the Bushman's light grass shelters leaning empty against banks of crimson sand: or one of his game-pits neatly dug, and the sands littered with the hair and bone of the animal. Once, some miles away from our camp, deep in the desert a fire suddenly flared up in the dark, was caught by the sterile west wind, and went flying past us like an overland night express. '*Massarwa*! Bushman!' the cry went up among our startled black companions. But as the weeks went by still we did not see him.

One evening, in a camp hurriedly pitched for shelter against the first violent storm of summer, I was watching the Gothic lightning strike at the reeling earth around us when, against a flash of flame on the horizon, I saw a movement above the line of bushes. I watched carefully and when the sheet-lightning flared purple in the smoking rain again I saw the silhouettes of two little heads peering intently at us.

Instantly I left the camp in the opposite direction, crept out into the storm, and worked my way around to the line of the bushes. I came out about thirty yards beyond the place I had marked. The noise of thunder, wind and rain was at its height and greatly helped me. I rose carefully. Between me and the light of our fires indeed were two little Bushman heads. I crept up quietly, suddenly put my hands on their shoulders, said loudly: 'Good day. I saw you from afar.'

The two little men fell over backwards with astonishment and, far from being upset, began laughing so much that they wriggled helplessly in the wet sand for a while unable to stand up. I took them into my camp and though none of us could speak their dialect we spent one of the happiest evenings I have ever known. I watched them eating the huge meal of roast springbuck, rice and raisins which my wonderful old safari cook and friend, Simon Marenga, a **Northern Rhodesian**, had cooked for us, and the sight of their pure Bushman faces and bodies sent a warm feeling to my heart. I looked forward to days of their company. But when morning came the pair had vanished and not a footprint left by wind and rain to show which way they had gone.

On another occasion, during a halt to mend a wheel, on a day of steel, two little hunters suddenly appeared like reflections in a distorting mirror on the far face of the shining ridge. They trotted easily towards us in the manner my aunt had described so well, and came straight into our midst holding out before them the buck-skins they wanted to exchange for tobacco. We took them on with us in our trucks for a while but again were unable to speak except by sign. The use and shape of our trucks was a complete puzzle to them so we had to lift them, like babies in arms, in and out of the vehicles. One of them, excited by a herd of buck he wanted to chase, hurled himself from the vehicle which was going at full speed to fall on to the sands, apparently knowing no other way of leaving it! Surprised, by signs, we asked if they never climbed the great desert trees to spy out game? They seemed astonished and indicated clearly that they would never do anything so unnecessary while the spoor of game was printed plainly in the sand for them to read. We then shot some game for them and saw them throw themselves, helpless with laughter, upon the sand when the first of the guns went off. As the sun began to sink, though we besought them to stay, they insisted on leaving us. I longed to accompany them but my mission was too exacting to allow it. Full of **chagrin** I watched

---

Northern Rhodesia: now Zambia
chagrin: frustration

them, each carrying a buck across his firm little shoulders, walk gracefully away from us into the sunset. One afternoon, on another expedition, at a time of terrible drought we came across the footprints of one grown-up person and two small children. The manner of the **spoor** perturbed me greatly. I showed it to my tracker. He confirmed my fears, saying: 'People in trouble.' Instantly we followed the spoor for six miles, while it became more faltering and desperate. At the edge of a great pan I felt certain it was made by people half-dead by thirst. We searched the hollow depression. It was waterless, and the dried-up mud in the bottom was cracked and dull like the scales of a dead fish. Then far away in the white flame of heat we saw three little blobs of brown fluttering like wounded birds. We found a Bushman woman with a baby strapped to her side and two little boys nearly dead of thirst staggering about. We gave them water. The woman drank nearly three gallons, though she was careful to ration the children. Again we could not speak her dialect and had to make signs to her inviting her to stay. However she steadfastly refused. As soon as she had eaten, she filled all the empty ostrich egg-shells she carried in a leather shawl with water. I offered to come with her but, in a fever of agitation, she signed refusal. Then, apparently fully recovered, she picked up her baby and set off with the little boys, to vanish into the sand and the bush on the far side of the pan.

In the years that followed I had other brief and tantalising encounters with the genuine Bushman. But I was too busy to pursue the matter independently to its own lawful conclusion. Instead I tried to persuade more fully qualified people, scientists, anthropologists and psychologists, to follow up this line of living research and go and live with the Bushman in order to find out,

---

spoor: trail (footprints etc.) which a hunter will follow to find his prey

before it was too late, his way of spirit and life. It seemed a strange paradox that everywhere men and women were busy digging up old ruins and buried cities in order to discover more about ancient man, when all the time the ignored Bushman was living with this early spirit still intact. I found men willing enough to come with me to measure his head, or his behind, or his sexual organs, or his teeth. But when I pleaded with the head of a university in my own country to send a qualified young man to live with the Bushman for two or three years, to learn about him and his ancient way, he exclaimed, surprised: 'But what would be the use of that? The Bushman would just fill him up with lies!'

So for many precious years I cast around to find someone with more than a sharply sided interest in the Bushman. But it was a vain search. Yet all over the world whenever I spoke of the Bushman a look of wonder would come into the eyes of ordinary people and I took heart from that. I believe one cannot fully know people and life unless one knows them also through the wonder they provoke in one. Without a sense of wonder one has lost not only the spoor of life but the power of true increase.

Increasingly, my own imagination became troubled with memories of the Bushman, and in particular with the vision of the set of footprints I had found in the pan in the central desert at the foot of a great storm-tree. It was almost as if those footprints were the spoor of my own lost self vanishing in the violet light of a desert of my own mind. I found myself compelled against my conscious will towards the conclusion that, ridiculous as it might seem, I myself ought perhaps to take up the spoor where it vanished in the sand. Then one morning I awoke to find that, in sleep, my mind had been decided for me.

'I will go and find the Bushman,' I told myself, suddenly amazed that so simple a statement had never presented itself to me before.

Activities

The search for Mallory and Irvine

1 How do the writers of this extract keep the reader wanting to read on and find out what happens? Complete a table like the one below by finding examples of each narrative device listed.

Narrative device	Example(s)
quoting what the mountaineers say (especially exclamations)	'Holy shit!' 'This isn't him . . .
vivid images	
detailed descriptions	
sudden revelation of evidence	
raising expectations, and then revealing the unexpected	
sharing the climbers' bafflement	
emphasising emotional response	
explaining the pressures of: • the need for speed • the dangers of the situation	
the climbers' empathy with their predecessors	

2 Write a playscript beginning at the moment when Conrad
Anker finds the body, and ending with the decision to look
for the camera and other possessions. Use all the words
spoken by the climbers as reported in the extract, and
make up the rest of the dialogue based on the descriptions
of the thoughts and actions of the climbers. The first few
lines have been given below, to start you off.

*Anker is waving excitedly. He points to the body as
Norton arrives. Norton hurriedly sits on a rock.*

NORTON   Holy shit!
ANKER   I never thought we'd find him today.
NORTON   I wasn't sure we'd find him at all!
Hahn joins them.
HAHN   Look at that! It's like a marble statue . . .

3 Are people who climb mountains or follow other
dangerous pursuits in search of 'firsts' or records (walking
across deserts, exploring deep caves etc.) heroic, or
completely mad? When things go wrong, should rescue
attempts be made, however difficult or dangerous? Or
should people who have accepted the risks involved in
these pursuits be left to their fate?

4 Now look at question 1 on page 157.

Skylla and Charybdis and In search of Scylla's Cave

Skylla and Charybdis

1 Which of the following words would you apply to Odysseus?

- *modest*   • *authoritative*   • *honest*   • *brave*

Explain why the words you have chosen apply, and why the others do not.

2 As a class, brainstorm clues that show the extract to be very old. What elements are present in the writing that you would not expect to find in a modern piece?

3 A *simile* is a comparison between two things – in this extract Odysseus compares the bubbling whirlpool Charybdis to 'a cauldron over a strong fire' (page 128)

An *epic simile* is a very long and complicated simile. There is one epic simile in this passage, on page 129. Find it, and explain the comparison being made.

In search of Scylla's Cave

4 There have been many attempts to discover the truth behind Greek myths and other legends. Should we treat legends as history, and try to find out the real events that gave rise to them? Or should we simply enjoy them as stories? Write notes for 3 arguments in favour of each point of view.

5 Is the author of this extract setting out with an open mind to discover the truth, or is he intent of proving a point? Explain your answer.

6 Now look at question 1 on page 157.

A brahmin picnic

1 Do you find out most about people's *character* or *behaviour* in this extract? Give an example to help support your answer.

2 Do you think that V.S. Naipaul sets out to observe people, or to get involved with them? Do events force him to change his role? If so, how and why?

3 Complete a table like the one below to show what aspects of the brahmins' behaviour disturb the author, and why.

What they do	Why the author is disturbed
Their leader lectures them	He knows the leader is talking nonsense
The old servant gives out food	

How does VS Naipaul behave towards his hosts and avoid giving offence?

4 Imaging you are an alien newly arrived on Earth, knowing nothing about its history or culture. You witness a typical ceremony or festival; because you don't understand you may feel embarrassed, upset or frightened. Write a report to your High Council reporting what you have seen.

Select an event from the following – or choose a different one which you are familiar with:

- making and serving a pot of tea
- queuing for a bus
- a wedding
- a cricket match

5 Now look at question 1 on page 157.

A witch trial in Orissa

1 What does the extract tell you about Tahir Shah, Bhalu the Trickster and the Headman of the village? Make brief notes on each character.

2 Tahir Shah uses some words in this extract that may be unfamiliar. Write down the following words from the third paragraph (pages 139–140) and write a more familiar word alongside them that means much the same thing:

Word used	Alternative	Word used	Alternative
fled	ran away	observed	
departed	left	transform	
resort		ancient	
pacing			

Re-read the paragraph, substituting the simpler words for the original ones. What effect does this have on the style? Can you suggest why Tahir Shah has chosen to use the words he has?

3 Work in pairs.

- One person must make a list of every piece of evidence that shows that the accused woman is **guilty**.
- The other person must write down all the evidence that the woman is **not guilty**.
- Each person then writes down a closing statement, which summarises all their evidence.

All the people arguing that the woman is **guilty** gather in one group, and those arguing that she is **not guilty** gather in another. Restage the trial with two prosecuting lawyers from one group and two defence lawyers from the other. The rest of the class will be witnesses and the teacher will be the judge.

4 Now look at question 1 on page 157.

Encounters with Bushmen

1 Do you think Laurens van der Post wanted to meet and understand the San for emotional or observational reasons? Give evidence from the text.

2 Compare the length of sentences in this extract with those in *A witch trial in Orissa* (page 139) and *The search for Mallory and Irvine* (page 119).

- What effect does the length of the author's sentences have on the style and tone of the piece?
- In what way does this style suit the subject matter of this extract?
- Does this piece have a modern, or an old-fashioned feel?

3 Complete a table like the one below. Note down significant details about the San's culture and behaviour:

Facts about the San	Evidence in the text
They are not upset at being caught out	They burst out laughing when the author creeps up
They do not like staying in one place	The first two San the author met were gone in the morning

4 Work in pairs. Imagine that you and your partner are the pair of San who meet Laurens van der Post in the first part of the extract, or the San woman in the second part explaining the meeting to a friend.

    a Discuss this meeting from your own point of view. Remember that you may never have been so close to a white person before.

    b Bring all the pairs together into a tribal gathering. Discuss the meetings you have had with the strangers. Are they a threat to your way of life? Can you be friends?

5 Now look at question 1 on page 157.

Comparing texts

1 Each piece of travel writing has a particular purpose. The **language** and **structure** of a piece of writing helps get this purpose across to the reader. For each extract in this section use a format like the one on page 194 (see a completed example on page 196) to write a report on how these pieces of travel writing achieve their effect.

2 Copy the table below.

Extract	Motivation	Evidence
Homer/Odysseus	to create a record of his journeys that people would marvel at.	Odysseus describes his journeys in chilling detail: he is always at the centre of the adventure.
Tim Severin	to prove his theory about the truth of Odysseus's voyages	
V.S. Naipaul		
Tahir Shah		
Laurens van der Post		
Hemmleb, Johnson and Simonson		

Why do you think each of the writers in this section decided to search for their roots, or for the origins of people who mattered to them? Complete the table on page 157. Explain, in your view, the main motive of each person. Give reasons for your answers.

3 Compare ONE of the extracts in this section with ONE of the extracts in Section 3 (pages 81–110). Which extract shows more personal involvement on the part of its author? Can you suggest why this might be?

4 Some of these writers are interested in individual people; some are interested in groups of people, and some are interested in both groups and individuals.

Write a report explaining which writers fall into which category, and your reasons for thinking so.

5 Which extract in this section did you find most interesting and involving? Did any extract not interest you? Use the reports you have completed to comment on the **text type**, **language**, **tone**, **narrator**, **address** and **period** of the extract(s) to help explain your response.

6 If you were able to undertake a quest to find out about the origins and history of a person or group of people, who would you choose? Why?

Write a **plan** for your quest. Explain:

- whose 'roots' you wish to discover
- what preparations you will need to make:
  - to research your subject
  - for the journey
- what location you will need to visit
- who you will need to speak to, or what records you will need to examine
- what will be the ultimate aim of your quest
- how you will record/report your quest.

Strange lands

Nowadays, travel by air is fast and cheap. A traveller can be almost anywhere on the planet within two or three days of leaving home.

It wasn't always like that; and even today, there are regions of the world that are remote and inaccessible. There are still mountains, deserts, rainforests, remote islands and snowy wastes where visitors are almost unknown.

The travellers that venture to such places do so for many reasons, but mainly to see what the world was like before the industrial countries tamed it with roads, railways, airports, cities and factories. Here are some of their experiences ...

Strange islands, stranger people

from The Travels of Sir John Mandeville

1322

by Sir John Mandeville

People didn't travel much in 1322. So, when Sir John Mandeville produced a book about his travels, people believed that what he wrote was the truth. However, there are one or two problems with 'Sir John'!

Firstly, nobody is sure who 'Sir John Mandeville' was. He says in the book that he is an English knight from

St Albans. This is possible, but many scholars have identified him as a man called Jean de Bourgogne, a doctor from Liège in what is now Belgium. Secondly, we can't know for sure whether 'Sir John Mandeville' actually travelled anywhere or not! He could have sat at home and based his travel writings on sailors' tall tales. Although some parts of his book are quite accurate descriptions of real places in the fourteenth century, he also claims to have visited places, and seen things, which we now know do not exist.

So, was he really an early tourist or just a good storyteller? Read his account, and judge for yourselves ...

I, John Mandeville, knight (albeit I be not worthy), that was born in England, in the town of St Albans, and passed the sea in the year of our Lord Jesu Christ, in 1322, in the day of **St Michael**; and hitherto have been long time over the sea, and have seen and gone through many diverse lands, and many provinces and kingdoms and isles; where dwell many diverse folks, and of diverse manners and laws, and of diverse shapes of men. Of which lands and isles I shall speak more plainly hereafter ...

The Legend of the Phoenix
In Egypt is the city of **Heliopolis**, that is to say, the city of the Sun. In that city there is a temple, made round after the shape of the Temple of Jerusalem. The priests of that temple have all their writings under the date of the fowl that is called phoenix; and there is none but one in all the world. And he cometh to burn himself upon the altar of that temple at the end of five hundred year; for so long he liveth. And at the five hundred years' end, the priests

---

St Michael's Day: Michaelmas (29 September)
Heliopolis: Now a suburb of Cairo, Egypt

array their altar honestly, and put thereupon spices and sulphur and other things that will burn lightly; and then the bird phoenix cometh and burneth himself to ashes. And the day next after, men find in the ashes a **worm**, and the second day next after, men find a bird **quick** and perfect; and the third next day after, he flieth his way. And so there is no more birds of that kind in all the world, but it alone, and truly that is a great miracle of God. And men may well liken that bird unto God, because that there is no God but one; and also, that our Lord arose from death to life the third day. This bird men see often-time fly in those countries; and he is not mickle more than [not much bigger than] an eagle. And he hath a crest of feathers upon his head more great than the peacock hath; and his neck is yellow; and his beak is coloured blue as ind [indigo]; and his wings be of purple colour, and his tail is barred across with green and yellow and red. And he is a full fair bird to look upon against the sun, for he shineth full gloriously and nobly.

The Dog-People

Men go by sea from isle to isle unto an isle that is called **Nacumera**, that is a great isle and good and fair. And it is in compass about more than a thousand mile. And all the men and women of that isle have hounds' heads, and they be called Cynoceptales. And they be full reasonable and of good understanding, save that they worship an ox for their God. And also every one of them beareth an ox of gold or of silver in his forehead, in token that they love well their God. And they go all naked save a little **clout**. They be great folk and well-fighting. And they have

---

worm: snake, dragon, or any kind of reptile

quick: alive (as in 'the quick and the dead' from the Creed)

Nacumera: the name of this, and all the islands mentioned by the author, seem to be fictitious   **clout**: loincloth

great targe [shield] that covereth all the body, and a spear in their hand to fight with. And if they take any man in battle, anon they eat him.

From this land men go to another isle that is called Silha. And it is well an 800 miles about. In that land is full much waste, for it is full of serpents, of dragons and of cockodrills, that no man dare dwell there. These cockodrills [crocodiles] be serpents, yellow and rayed above, and have four feet and short thighs, and great nails as claws or talons. And there be some that have five **fathoms** in length, and some of six and of eight and of ten. And when they go by places that be gravelly, it seemeth as though men had drawn a great tree through the gravelly place. And there be also many wild beasts, and namely of elephants.

---

fathoms: measurement, approximately 6 feet or a little less than 2 metres

In that country and others there-about there be wild geese that have two heads. And there be lions, all white and as great as oxen, and many other diverse beasts and fowls also that be not seen amongst us.

In one of these isles be folk of great stature, as giants. And they be hideous for to look upon. And they have but one eye, and that is in the middle of the front. And they eat nothing but raw flesh and raw fish.

And in another isle toward the south dwell folk of foul stature and of cursed kind that have no heads. And their eyes be in their shoulders.

And in another isle be folk that have the face all flat, all plain, without nose and without mouth. But they have two small holes, all round, instead of their eyes, and their mouth is flat also without lips.

And in another isle be folk of foul fashion and shape that have the lip above the mouth, so great that when they sleep in the sun they cover all the face with that lip. And in another isle there be little folk, as dwarfs. And they be two so much [twice as large] as the pigmies. And they have no mouth; but instead of their mouth they have a little round hole, and when they shall eat or drink, they take through a pipe or a pen [quill] or such thing, and suck it in, for they have no tongue, and therefore they speak not, but they make a manner of hissing as an adder doth, and they make signs one to another **as monks do**, by the which every of them understandeth other.

And in another isle be folk that have great ears and long, that hang down to their knees.

And in another isle be folk that have horses' feet. And they be strong and mighty, and swift runners; for they take wild beasts with running, and eat them.

---

as monks do: monks from 'silent' orders were not allowed to speak, and so devised signs to communicate with each other

The Griffins

From that land go men toward the land of Bacharia where be full evil folk and full cruel. In that land be trees that bear wool, as though it were of sheep, whereof men make clothes and all things that may be made of wool.

In that country be many hippotaynes that dwell sometime in the water and sometime on the land. And they be half man and half horse, as I have said before. And they eat men when they may take them.

And there be rivers of waters that be **full bitter**, three times more than is the water of the sea.

In that country be many griffins, more plenty than in any other country. Some men say that they have the body upward as an eagle and beneath as a lion; and truly they **say sooth**, that they be of that shape. But one griffin hath the body more great and is more strong than eight lions, of such lions as be on this half, and more great and stronger than an hundred eagles such as we have amongst us. For one griffin there will bear, flying to his nest, a great horse, if he may find him at the point, or two oxen yoked together as they go at the plough. For he hath talons so long and so large and great upon his feet, as though they were horns of great oxen or of bugles [young bulls] or of **kine**, so that men make cups of them to drink of. And of their ribs and of the pens [pinions] of their wings, men make bows, full strong, to shoot with arrows.

After this, beyond the vale, is a great isle, where the folk be great giants of twenty-eight foot long, or of thirty foot long. And they have no clothing but of skins of beasts that they hang upon them. And they eat no bread, but all raw flesh; and they drink milk of beasts, for they have

---

full bitter: full of salt
say sooth: tell the truth
kine: cows

plenty of all bestial. And they have no houses to lie in. And they eat more gladly man's flesh than any other flesh. Into that isle dare no man gladly enter. And if they see a ship and men therein, anon they enter into the sea for to take them.

And men said us, that in an isle beyond that were giants of greater stature, some of forty-five foot, or of fifty foot long, and as men say, some of fifty **cubits** long. But I saw none of those for I had no **lust** to go to those parts, because that no man cometh neither into that isle nor into the other but that he be devoured **anon**. And among those giants be sheep as great as oxen here, and they bear great wool and rough. Of the sheep I have seen many times. And men have seen, many times, those giants take men in the sea out of their ships, and bring them to land, two in one hand and two in another, eating them as they go, all raw and alive.

Another isle is there toward the north, in the sea Ocean, where that be full cruel and full evil women of nature. And they have precious stones in their eyen. And they be of that kind, that if they behold any man with wrath they slay him anon **with the beholding**, as doth the **basilisk**.

And I John Mandeville, knight, abovesaid (although I be unworthy), that departed from our countries and passed the sea, the year of grace 1322, that have passed many lands and many isles and countries, and searched many full strange places, and have been in many a full good honourable company, and at many a fair deed of

---

cubit: measurement, approximately the length of an adult's forearm
lust: wish or desire
anon: immediately
with the beholding: by looking at him
basilisk: legendary reptile that could kill with its breath, or with a look

arms, (albeit that I did none myself, **for mine unable insuffisance**), now that I am come home **maugre myself**, to rest, **for gouts artetykes that me distrain** that define the end of my labour; against my will (God knoweth).

And thus, taking solace in my wretched rest, recording the time past, I have fulfilled these things, and put them written in this book, as would come into my mind, the year of grace 1356, in the thirty-fourth year that I departed from our countries. Wherefore I pray to all the readers and hearers of this book, if it please them, that they will pray to God for me and I shall pray for them.

Amen! Amen! Amen!

---

for mine unable unsuffisance: because I was not strong enough
maugre myself: against my will
for gouts artetyke that me distrain: Mandeville is suffering from a painful illness that makes further travels impossible

A narrow escape from a polar bear

from My Life as an Explorer
by Roald Amundsen (1872–1928)

The Norwegian explorer Roald Amundsen spent most of his life in the Arctic and Antarctic regions. He was the man who beat Captain Scott to the South Pole in 1911 and also spent several months trapped in a boat in the Arctic.

He wrote several books about his adventures. In this extract, Amundsen writes about his 1918 expedition to cross the North-east Passage and tells how he almost met a sticky end ...

We made the **lee** of the islets and tied up to the land ice two hundred yards from the beach. We named this rather uncertain haven Maud Harbour, and in spite of its unfavourable first aspect, it sheltered us safely for a year . . .

The searching Arctic winds are the greatest handicap to comfort in winter quarters, so our next enterprise was to shovel snow against the sides of the *Maud* until we had piled up a snow bank all around her nearly to the deck level and sloping steeply downward to the level of the ice. For convenience we made a gangplank at an easier grade, in such a manner as to make a runway leading from the ice up to the deck of the *Maud* at the point nearest to the door to the cabin. One side of this runway was provided with a rope hand rail to which, in slippery weather, one could cling to keep from falling.

One of the dogs was a female who was expecting shortly to have a litter. She was very fond of me, and every morning when I came out of the cabin she would

---

lee: the side sheltered from the wind

come running to me to be petted. I would pick her up in my arms and carry her down the runway to the ice so that she could accompany me on the morning walk which I took to keep in good condition. One morning, when I had got her in my arms and was just about to start down the runway, Jacob, the watchdog of the *Maud*, came running toward me and bumped against me so that my feet went out from under me and I plunged headlong down the steep slope at the side of the runway, landing on my right shoulder with the weight of my whole body on top of it. For a few moments I saw stars. When I came to, I managed to sit up on the ice, but found that my shoulder was giving me excruciating pain. I had no doubt it was a bad fracture, as X-rays three years later proved was the case. I succeeded in climbing aboard again and into my cabin. Here Wisting, who had studied first aid at a hospital in Oslo, did his best to get the fracture set. The pain was so intense and the swelling so bad that neither he nor I could tell at the time whether he had succeeded. I was so entirely knocked out by the shock that I kept my bed for eight days. Then I got Wisting to put my arm in a sling and started going about again. But my bad luck was not yet through with me.

On 8 November I came up on deck so early in the morning that it was still almost as dark as night. A fog added to the gloom. Jacob, the watchdog, came running to me, and after leaping about me in demonstrative fashion for some moments, dashed down the runway and disappeared off on the ice. I did not venture to follow him for fear of another fall, so made my way down the gangway and proceeded alongside the ship, watching carefully to avoid the ice and snow pieces that littered this passage. I had stood below the bow for only a moment when I heard a faint sound so odd that I pricked up my ears to listen better. It seemed like the first faint soughing of the wind in the rigging when a breeze springs up. In a moment it grew louder and was clearly the sound of heavy breathing. Straining my eyes in the direction from which it came, I finally **discerned** Jacob headed for the ship at the best pace he could muster, and the next instant I saw behind him the huge form of a Polar bear in hot pursuit. It was the breathing of this bear approaching rapidly that I had heard.

Instantly I realised the situation. This was a mother bear with her cub. Jacob had found them and teased the cub. The mother's fury had quickly decided Jacob that he had urgent business on board the ship. The situation had its humorous side, but I did not pause to enjoy that, because I saw it also had its dangers for me. When the bear saw me she sat down and gazed at me. I certainly did the same at her. However, I think our feelings were different. We were both at about the same distance from the gangway. What should I do? I was alone – no assistance – only one arm – the left. Well, I had not much choice. I started to run as quickly as possible for the gangplank, but the bear did the same thing. Now started a race between a healthy, furious bear and an invalid. Not much chance for the latter. As soon as I reached the gangway and turned to run on board, the bear stretched me to the ground with a well-aimed blow on my back. I fell on my broken arm – face down – and expected to be finished right away. But no – my lucky star had not stopped shining yet. Jacob, who had been on board all this time, took suddenly into his head to return – probably to play with the cub. In doing so, he had to pass where mother bear was busy with me. When she saw Jacob passing, she jumped high in the air and left me for Jacob. It did not take me long to get up and disappear into safety. It was one of the narrowest escapes of my life.

---

discerned: made out

Ancient stronghold of a murderous brotherhood

from Valleys of the Assassins
by Freya Stark

In modern English, an assassin is someone who kills for political or financial reasons.

The original Assassins were a fanatical sect of Islam, founded in the eleventh century by Hasan-i-Sabbah. They lived in secret bases in the mountains of Persia (now Iran). Before they went out to fight their enemies, they smoked hashish. This is how they got their name.

Later, the Assassins became professional murderers. They were led by a Grand Master, known as 'the Old Man of the Mountains', and were feared throughout the Middle East.

In 1930, the English traveller Freya Stark set out to visit the great stronghold of the Assassins, the Rock of Alamut.

Hasan-i-Sabbah joined the sect in the year A.D. 1071. He was to become the first Grand Master of the Assassins.

He brought a new idea into the political science of his day and treated murder **as the suffragette the hunger strike**, turning it into an avowed political weapon.

Even in his own lifetime it brought him power which spread from north Persia to the Mediterranean. The secret garden where he drugged and attached to himself

---

as the suffragette the hunger strike: women from the suffragette movement starved themselves, sometimes to death, as a protest at not being given the vote

his followers became known through the Crusaders' chronicles in Europe, giving us our word of Assassin, or Hashishin.

(Later, the Assassins) degenerated into professional murderers. In those days, their crimes used to be paid for in advance; if they survived, they enjoyed their earnings, which otherwise went to support their families. But (their descendants) are now quiet country people, and talk freely of anything except their religion. The Assassins' valley and the Rock of Alamut no longer know their ancient lords.

I had long wished to go there. But there were obstacles. One of them was that I could not find it on my map.

By dint of enquiries, I learned that Alamut has been visited eight or nine times at least by Europeans. One crosses the Talaghan range and reaches the Alamut River; and the castle is at a place called Qasir Khan on the left. That was as much as I knew: and with that I packed my bed and saddle-bags one May morning and started out with a Persian and two veiled ladies and a little girl, who were returning home.

The day was fine; our party friendly. At noon we lunched by the roadside among young poplars, and bought eggs from an old man sitting in the dust. My fellow-travellers had been to a brother's funeral: they were now taking his small child home to marry their little boy later on: they would send her to school first, they said.

'In our country, if you marry them too young their children die,' said I, trying to do the best I could for the little bride. She was seven years old.

'We shall wait another five years,' said they.

In the late afternoon we reached the foot of our first range. Our mules had only walked for five hours, an easy first day's stage, but the solitude and the slow dreamlike travelling in the sun already made it seem as if we were remote from the world's business in some little backwater of time.

Then we began to meet the stream of traffic which carries the Caspian rice across these passes. The rice is mentioned in a Chinese report of the second century, and is still carried along its ancient ways. The men came striding down with their laden mules behind them. Their white **frieze** coats, fastened on one side, were wrapped tightly against the cold; the straight-stemmed Kurdish pipe stuck in their sashes; their henna'd red beards were trimmed short in the Moslem way. They had squarer faces than the townsfolk, with open brows and longish nose, straight or slightly curved, but not **aquiline**. They greeted us with jovial friendly greetings; looked at me wonderingly; and welcomed me to their country.

The small bells tied at the mules' hindquarters tinkled pleasantly through the still morning air as the long trains came down the zig-zag path. And after three and a half hours we came by the source of the stream; and after that to the long whale's back of the ridge; and looked on the country below.

This is a great moment, when you see, however distant, the goal of your wandering. The thing which has been living in your imagination suddenly becomes a part of the tangible world. It matters not how many ranges, rivers or parching dusty ways may lie between you; it is yours now for ever.

There was the Assassins' valley, tilted north-eastward: before it, among lower ridges, the Shah Rud showed a gleaming bend. Beyond and higher than all, uplifted as an altar with black ridges to it through snowfields, Takht-i-Suleiman, Solomon's throne, looked like a throne indeed

---

frieze: heavy woollen material
aquiline: hooked

in the great circle of its lesser peers. A story has it that King Solomon, having married the Queen of Sheba, could in no wise make her love him. He was old and she was young. He tried every inducement in vain, and at last he sent out the birds of the air and charged them to discover for him the coldest place in the world. Next morning at dawn all returned except the hoopoe, who remained absent all day. As the dusk was falling he too flew back and bowed before the king, and told him the cause of his delay. He had found a summit so cold that, when he alighted, his wings were frozen to the ground, and only the midday sun had been able to thaw them: and he had hastened to give the news to the king.

On the top of this mountain. Solomon built his bed, and took Belkeis the queen, and when the cold of night descended she could not bear it, but crept into her husband's tent. In the morning, King Solomon touched the rocky slope, and a warm spring gushed out for her to bathe in. And it remains to this day.

This is the story, and the mountain is still called the throne of Solomon, Takht-i-Suleiman. Its white drapery shone with the starched and flattened look of melting snow in the distance. The black rock arms of the chair were sharp against the sky.

The great Rock of Alamut looks a grim place. Mount Haudegan behind it rises in shady slopes with granite precipices above. A green patch high up shows a small spring whence, said the guide, with obliging inventiveness, the castle's water supply was drawn in **conduits**. East and west of the rock, far below, run the two streams that form the Qasir Rud; they eat their way through scored and naked beds. There is no green of grass until, beyond a neck that joins the castle to this desolate background, one climbs under its eastern lee,

conduits: pipes, channels

reaches the level by old obliterated steps, and from the southern end looks down nearly a thousand feet of stone to the fields and trees of Qasir Khan.

Here from some buttress in the castle wall, Hasan-i-Sabbah could watch for the return of his **Fedawis**. Here, no doubt, he would look out for his messengers when armies came against him; and from here perhaps saw the messengers coming to say that the Assassins' work was done. Here as an old man he might stroll in the last sunlight and look on his lands already in shadow, peaceful below him with their crops. The place was now covered with wild tulips, yellow and red, among the stones and mortar. Patches of wall clung here and there to the lip of the rock and showed the extent of the enclosure: but nearly everything is ruined beyond the power of imagination to reconstruct.

Fedawis: warriors

Cannibalism and cargo cults
from The Happy Isles of Oceania
by Paul Theroux

Paul Theroux is one of the best known and most popular modern travel writers. In this book, he describes a canoe journey along the Pacific island chains of Polynesia and Melanesia. Until quite recently, there were cannibals in the islands; and some of the islanders are followers of 'cargo cults'.

Years ago, when an island that had no contact with the outside world was visited by a plane or a ship, it sometimes happened that the people who lived on the island would mistake the travellers for gods – especially when the strangers brought 'magical' gifts (such as glass beads or mirrors). After the travellers left, the islanders would forget what actually happened, and the whole episode would pass into legend. Sometimes the islanders would build images in the shape of an aeroplane or ship out of wood and creepers, to try to persuade the 'gods' to visit again and bring more amazing gifts. They would have created a 'cargo cult'.

I had found circumstantial evidence for cannibalism – the liking in Vanuatu (and it had been the case in the Solomons too) for Spam. It was a theory of mine that former cannibals of Oceania now feasted on Spam because Spam came the nearest to approximating to the porky taste of human flesh. 'Long pig', as they called a cooked human being in much of Melanesia. It was a fact that the people-eaters of the Pacific had all evolved, or perhaps degenerated, into Spam-eaters. And in the absence of Spam they settled for corned beef, which also had a corpsy flavor.

But cannibalism was less interesting to me than cargo cults. Most of all I wanted to visit Tanna because I had heard that a cargo cult, the Jon Frum Movement, flourished on the island. The villagers in this movement worshipped an obscure, perhaps mythical, American named Jon Frum who was supposed to have come to Tanna in the 1930s. He appeared from nowhere and promised the people an earthly paradise. All they had to do was reject Christian missionaries and go back to their old ways. This they did with enthusiasm – booting out the Presbyterians. Jon Frum had not so far returned. The Jon Frum villages displayed a wooden red cross, trying to lure him – and his cargo of free goods – to the island. This iconography of the cross was not Christian, but rather derived from the war, from the era of free food and Red Cross vehicles.

The believers sat in hot little box-like structures and prayed to Jon Frum. Some had visions of the strange American. They sang Jon Frum ditties in Bislama, the local **Pidgin**.

Chief Tom Namake had returned from his trip to the bush. He had a fat sweaty face and a big belly. He spoke quickly – so quickly he sounded as though he was being evasive. He wore a dirty T-shirt that said *Holy Commando*, with the motif of an archer, and motto from Isaiah 49:2, *He made me into a polished arrow*.

'I have just come from Yakel,' I said.

'What do you think?'

I hesitated and then said, 'Were those people cannibals at one time?'

'Oh, yes,' Chief Tom said, and seemed pleased to be disclosing it. 'Many people were cannibals. But cannibalism on Tanna stopped about a hundred years ago. It was

---

Pidgin: a sort of shorthand second language understood among communities that all speak different first languages

mostly over land disputes that they killed and ate each other. The Big Nambas were the last people to be cannibals. If you promise not to write it down I will tell you a true cannibal story.'

'Why can't I write it?'

'You will take my magic if you do! Don't fool with such things! Oh, I don't think I will tell you after all.'

'Please,' I said. 'Look, no pen, No paper.'

Chief Tom regarded all writing with alarm, because it was a way of stealing someone's magic. I understood exactly what he meant, and I agreed with him. It was a fact, not a savage superstition. If he told a story, and I wrote it down, the story became mine. I did not have the guts to tell Chief Tom that writing was my business.

Wiping his hands on his *Holy Commando* shirt, he began.

'It was just down the road here, near Imanaka village, about a hundred years ago. A certain European trader came in a ship looking for – what? Some things – food, water, what-not.

'The Tanna people saw him at the beach. They listened to him and said they could help him. They tell him to follow them and still talk to him in a friendly way, and when they get down into the bush they take out bush knives and kill him, then stab him with spears. He is dead.

'They carry him to their village and prepare the fire and the stones for the oven to cook him. And then they take his clothes off. One man feels the arm and says, "I like this – I eat this!" And another says, "I want this leg."

'And another and another, and so on, until they have the whole body divided, except the feet.

'The last man says, "I want these" – meaning the feet.'

Chief Tom smiled and smacked his lips and poked his thick black forefinger into my chest.

'The dead man is wearing canvas shoes!' he cried. 'They never seen canvas shoes before! They take the shoes off and say, "Hey, hey! This must be the best part!" So they throw the body away and keep the shoes. They boil them for a while, then they try to eat them, the canvas shoes!'

I interrupted at this point and said, 'I don't understand why they threw the body away.'

'Because it is nothing to them, but the feet you can remove – that is special.'

'The feet you can remove are the shoes, right?'

'They never see such things before,' Chief Tom said. 'That is why they boil them. After they take them out of the pot they chew and chew. Cannot even bite the canvas shoes. They try to tear them with their teeth. No good.

'Everyone has a chew.

'"What is this? Cannot eat his feet!"

'They take the shoes to another village and those ones try to eat the canvas shoes, but it is impossible.

'So they dig a big hole and throw in the canvas shoes and cover them. Then they plant a coconut tree on top of it. That tree grew up very tall – and when the storm came in eighty-seven it blew the tree down, so they planted another tree. It is still growing. I can show you the tree tomorrow.'

Looking for the cannibal palm and the burial place of the canvas shoes late on one hot afternoon, I discovered a wonderful thing: Imanaka was a Jon Frum village – there was the red cross, in wood, at the centre of the lopsided woven huts. A cargo cult flourished within.

Imanaka, wreathed in smoke from cooking fires, was in the woods, on a stony hillside, behind a broken fence, at the end of a muddy track. It was easy to see how such a hard-up village would take to the idea of deliverance and develop faith in the idea that one day an immense amount of material goods would come their way, courtesy of Jon Frum, only if they believed in him and danced and sang his praises. But it was also an article of faith that Jon Frum villages had to neglect their gardens and throw their money away: when Jon Frum returned he would provide everything.

The chief, whose name was Yobas, was old and feeble, carrying a stick that was smooth where his hand gripped it. He wore a torn undershirt and dirty cloth tied like a sarong, and he had the oppressed and wincing expression of a chief who was probably being blamed by everyone, including his own people, for presiding over such a miserable village.

'*Yu savvy tok Inglis?*'

Incredibly, he nodded: yes, he did.

I greeted him by making an insincere speech saying what a delightful village it was and how happy I was to be in it, and I hoped that this would put all thoughts of killing me out of their minds.

'So this is a Jon Frum village?'

'Yiss. All dis. Jon Frum.' And he motioned with his stick.

'The village dances for Jon Frum?'

'We dance here' – it seemed that we were sitting in the open-sided dance hall. 'For Jon Frum. Also sing-sing. For Jon Frum.'

'Sometimes do you see Jon Frum?'

'Nuh. But the old fella they see him.'

'What does Jon Frum look like? Is he black or white?'

'White like you. From America. He is a beeg man – very fat! He strong!'

'What does he wear?'

'He wear clothes. He wear everything. He wear hat.'

I was wearing a baseball hat. I said, 'Like this?'

'Nuh. Big hat. Like a missionary.'

I took out my notebook and drew a picture of a wide-brimmed hat. He said, Yes, that's the one. And when he spoke the other men and the children crowded around me and jostled for a look at the notebook page.

Gesturing at the thatched shelter, I said, 'You sing-sing here?'

'Yiss. We sing-sing.'

'Please. Sing-sing for me.'

The old chief considered this, and then hitched himself forward and in a whispering voice that rustled and hissed like tissue paper he began to sing.

Jon Frum
He mus come
Look at old fellas
Give us some big presents
Give us some good tok-tok

He looked squarely at me and rolled his head and whispered again,

Jon Frum
He mus come.

Was Jon Frum a friendly American pilot who had brought supplies here and shared them around? And perhaps he had said, *I am John from America*. And then had the war convinced the villagers on Tanna how wealthy America was?

It hardly mattered now. The dogma of the movement seemed to suggest that Jon Frum was a sort of John the Baptist, preceding the saviour, who was a redeemer in the form of cargo – every nice and useful object imaginable. And the important aspect was that it had come to the island directly, without the help of missionaries or interpreters. No money, no tithing was involved; no Ten Commandments, no Heaven or Hell. No priests, nor any imperialism. It was a Second Coming, but it enabled the villagers to rid themselves of missionaries and live their lives as they had before. It seemed to me a wonderfully foxy way of doing exactly as they pleased.

Holidays in space
from *The Guardian*

Will travel become so easy that we can go anywhere on Earth we want to? If it does how can people 'get away from it all'? Here's one possible solution ...

Holidays in space won't help to cure the earth's problems. **George Monbiot** intends to keep his feet on the ground

On another planet

A few years before he died, **Bruce Chatwin** recalled a conversation with a Moslem hermit in a North African Desert. 'There is a people called the Mericans?' the hermit asked him. 'There is.' 'They say they have visited the Moon.' 'They have.' 'They are blasphemers.'

The hermit had a point.

As the earth staggers under its load, the world's richest nations have spent tens of billions of dollars and deployed some of the finest scientific minds in discovering not how to save it, but how to get off it. This extraordinary planet, this place in which, perhaps uniquely, the freak conditions required to

Bruce Chatwin: art expert, journalist, traveller and novelist, who died in 1989 at the age of 49

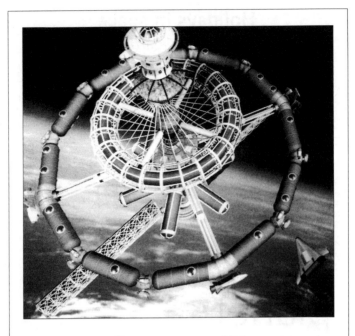

sustain life are all present, is seen by the pioneers of space travel merely as a stepping stone to other worlds. As the rich and powerful fantasise about escaping, their incentive to invest in protecting our own planet dwindles.

The warped dreams of the armchair astronauts may now be a little more attainable. The Artemis Project, which describes itself as 'a private venture to establish a permanent, self-supporting community on the Moon', promises that, within the foreseeable future, it will be shuttling tourists between the Earth and its satellite.

This scheme's backers may be living on another planet, but less ambitious space tourism ventures are beginning to look feasible. The notion of orbiting the earth for fun, once the domain of sad technofantasists, is now the province of sad techno-realists. A consortium of millionaires called the X Prize Foundation has offered a \$10 million reward to the first company to build a passenger craft capable of flying in orbit 100km from the earth, using only private money. It won't be long before someone claims it.

Zegrahm Expeditions, based in Seattle, has been taking deposits for a 'space-plane' venture which, it, maintains, will be launched on 1 December 2001. Buzz Aldrin, who walked on the moon with Neil Armstrong and is now the spokesperson for a speculative space tourism company, claims that 'by October 2000 we should be sending up a journalist who can tell people in a professional way what it's like to go into space. Then every six months or so, Nasa should make space available, a seat on the shuttle, for regular people to go into orbit.'

His company, he suggests, will ferry people out to 'space hotels'. Already, a Japanese firm called Shimizu Corporation has published plans for a sort of interplanetary Butlins, where tourists will be able to play space sports and gaze on our workaday planet with pity. An organisation called Space Future foresees three stages of space tourism: the 'pioneering phase', during which a small number of passengers will pay astronomical fees to be the first to enjoy an out-of-this-world holiday; a 'mature phase', catering for hundreds of thousands every year; and a 'mass phase', during which ticket prices will drop to the cost of a sea cruise and millions of people will be able to travel. 'Ultimately,' the organisation claims, space is 'the future of the human race – or did you think there was somewhere else to go?'

Well, we certainly won't be able to stay here if these enterprises get their way. None of these companies envisage Apollo-type launches for their spacecraft, in which a disposable rocket sits on top of a great tower of fuel, but the shuttles they are designing will still require a formidable quantity of hydrocarbons to get into orbit. Everything the tourists need – the materials to build the hotels and the air, food, water and fuel required to keep their guests alive – will have to be lifted into orbit. If the space tourism industry is not to be jeopardised by flying debris, then all the waste they produce will have to be brought back down.

It is hard to think of a better designed project for maximum environmental destruction. If the industry takes off as some of its boosters would like us to believe, it will rapidly become the world's primary source of carbon dioxide emissions. In our quest to populate the barren interplanetary wastes, we threaten to lay waste to the only life-sustaining planet astronomers have been able to detect.

Doubtless space tourism agencies will seek to make us feel inadequate and dull if we choose to stay behind. They will broker the dissatisfaction that holiday companies trade in today when trying to persuade people to visit India or the US. We will go, as we go on intercontinental journeys, in the hope of finding something that we have never defined in the course of a quest we have never examined. And, as ever, the thing we are looking for will be inside us all along.

Activities

Strange islands, stranger people . . .

1 Which parts of this extract do you think are fact and which fantasy? Complete a table like the one below:

Real people/creatures	Fantasy people/creatures
serpents (snakes)	the phoenix
cockodrills (crocodiles)	dragons

2 English has changed since the author wrote his book more than six hundred years ago. List the words and phrases that are no longer in everyday use. Then write down a modern equivalent of each word.

Mandeville's word	Modern equivalent
albeit	although
hitherto	from that day to this
diverse	different
dwell	
hereafter . . .	

3 Look at the extract and make a list of:

- legendary creatures e.g. the phoenix
- made up creatures e.g. the dog-people
- things that really exist but that Mandeville doesn't understand as we do e.g. 'trees that bear wool'. What do you think he is describing?

4 Write a brief description in modern English of the phoenix, a griffin and one of the people or creatures of the islands as the author describes them.

5 Now look at question 1 on page 190.

A narrow escape from a polar bear

1 Roald Amundsen wrote about this adventure over seventy years ago when correct, formal English was the accepted style of writing. Match the phrases below in today's English with phrases in the extract.

  a although it didn't look very good at first
  b the cold winds at the North Pole made living there in winter very uncomfortable
  c jumping up to show how happy he was to see me
  d I didn't try to go after him; I was afraid I might fall again
  e as fast as he could possibly go

2 **Working in groups**, find and examine a few stories featuring narrow escapes in recent copies of popular tabloid newspapers (the *Sun*, *Daily Star*, *Mirror* etc.). You will need to do some research beforehand. Compare their style of reporting with Amundsen's. Make a list of features of tabloid reporting styles and share your findings.

As a class, produce an agreed list of features that are common to the style of tabloid newspaper reporting.

3 Imagine you are a tabloid newspaper reporter. Write a newspaper article based on the second part of Amundsen's story (from page 168 paragraph 4 – 'On 8th November . . .'). Use this example to start you off.

> ## BEAR BIFFS BOFFIN!
>
> NUTTY NORWEGIAN scientist and explorer Roald Amundsen nearly came to a sticky end this week. The silly Scandinavian had already:
>
> * got his ship caught in the ice
> * come a cropper on an icy gangplank and
> * broken his shoulder
>
> when he

4 Now look at question 1 on page 190.

Ancient stronghold of a murderous brotherhood

1 Imagine you are an Assassin. Write out an advertisement, based on the information in the extract, for the Jobs Wanted pages of your local newspaper. Set out:

   a what skills you have to offer
   b what terms and conditions of employment you expect.

2 Match the phrases below in today's English with phrases in the extract.

   a they were the only people at that time who had no prejudices about religion
   b from which, said the guide, making up stories in an effort to be helpful
   c everything is so completely destroyed that it is impossible to guess what it must have been like.

3 Use the evidence in the extract to predict the meaning of:

   Hashishin (page 171, paragraph 1)
   Rud (page 172, paragraph 5)
   Takht (page 173, paragraph 3)

4 In 1190, King Richard the Lionheart and his allies set off from Europe in a Crusade to 'free' the Holy Land. The Crusaders were constantly harried by the Assassins, and thought that the Assassins were terrorists. Working in pairs, make brief notes on the following:

   • Discover which groups today use murder as a political weapon, like the Assassins. Research materials from newspapers, TV and radio news and the Internet, and make a list of conflicts in which one side or the other (or both) are using terror tactics to try to gain a political advantage.
   • Is there a difference between a terrorist and a freedom-fighter? Does it depend which side you're on?
   • Can such behaviour be justified in a desperate situation? Or is there no excuse for murder in any circumstances?

5 Now look at question 1 on page 190.

Cannibalism and cargo cults

1 Which of the descriptions best matches the writer's attitude to:

- Chief Tom Namake
- the Chief of Imanaka?

a liking and respect
b tolerant amusement
c scorn and distrust

Explain your answers.

2 Which of these statements correctly explains Chief Tom Namake's attitude to the Tanna cannibals? He thinks they were:

a wicked because they killed the European trader.
b wicked because they wanted to eat a human being.
c foolish because they did not know what canvas shoes were.

Explain your answer.

3 How can we tell that the writer's account of his journey to the Pacific Islands is more recent than the previous two extracts? Make notes demonstrating that this is the case, under the following headings:

- References to contemporary things, people and events
- Length of sentences
- Descriptions of people and places
- Dialogue
- Use of slang words and expressions

For each heading,

- provide evidence from the text *and*
- explain its significance.

4 Now look at question 1 on page 190.

Holidays in space?

1 Summarise each paragraph of the article as briefly as possible. The first two paragraphs have been done for you:

Paragraph	Summary
1	Some people think space travel is wrong and unnatural
2	The richest people are more interested in getting off the Earth than saving it, so they have no reason to look after the planet.
3	

2 a When you have completed your summary, explain how the writer has constructed his argument. Which of the following conclusions does he wish the reader to reach?
- that humankind has a future in space
- that we should celebrate the successes of space travel
- that people should take space travel seriously
- that there are serious dangers to the environment in unrestricted space travel.

3 **Debate**
Divide the class into two groups; one will argue that space travel is the future of humankind; the other, that space travel is a costly waste of time. Each group should research material to back up its arguments. Evidence should include the history of space exploration, current events in space exploration and speculative articles (such as this one).

Those arguing in favour of space travel may find useful material on the websites of organisations such as the British Interplanetary Society and NASA, those against on the websites of environmental protection organisations such as Greenpeace (see Further Reading, page 199).

Hold a debate on this question.

4 Now look at question 1 on page 190.

Comparing texts

1 Each piece of travel writing has a particular purpose. The **language** and **structure** of a piece of writing helps get this purpose across to the reader. For each extract in this section use a format like the one on page 194 (see a completed example on page 196) to write a report on how these pieces of travel writing achieve their effect.

2 Match each author's name to the description of the type of writing that most closely matches the extract that appears in this section:

a	Roald Amundsen	**i**	description of a journey
b	Freya Stark	**ii**	delivering information and a warning
c	Paul Theroux	**iii**	examination of human behaviour
d	George Monbiot	**iv**	descriptions of an event

3 How does the narrative viewpoint of George Monbiot in *Holidays in space?* differ from that of the other extracts in this section? What is the effect of this different viewpoint?

4 Compare any two of the above extracts. Use the questionnaires you have completed to comment on the **text type**, **language**, **tone**, **narrator**, **address** and **period** of each extract, in order to show how each uses a different style to achieve its purpose.

5 Rewrite Roald Amundsen's extract in the style suggested. Make sure you use the features that you have identified as belonging to that style.

Extract	Rewrite in the style of
A narrow escape from a polar bear (pages 167–169)	→ **Holidays in space?** (pages 181–184) (Turn Roald Amundsen's story into **a** warning of the foolishness of a polar exploration and **b** messing around with an enraged polar bear.)

6 Imagine that you are a person from a far-off place, for whom the country you live in is a 'strange land.' Choose one of the styles in this section to write about an aspect of your own country, or its people, as it might be viewed by an outsider.

You might choose to write about:

- An encounter with a 'dangerous' animal (in the style of Roald Amundsen)
- A visit to a place of historical importance (in the style of Freya Stark)
- A warning that some activity pursued by the inhabitants will lead to disaster (in the style of George Monbiot).

Remember to include the features that you have studied for that style, and to:

- **describe people, places and events fully and carefully**, as your readers will be no more familiar with what you are describing than you are;
- **concentrate your attention on the aspect you have chosen**, and give any information on the environment, history or behaviour of the local inhabitants that your readers might find useful.

Make sure that you use:

- headings
- paragraphs
- complete sentences.

Epilogue

We'll leave the last word to John Hatt, a traveller who has clearly been there, done that, and got the T-Shirt . . .

Sound advice

So pack your bags and go on your travels before it is too late. There are still vast tracts of the world which beg to be visited; and travel will give you a wealth of experience and pleasure which can be drawn on for the rest of your life – a wealth, futhermore, which no government can ever take away. If the very worst happens and you are miserable on your travels (unlikely), at least you will have learnt to appreciate your own country. I have never regretted visiting a single country (though three days in Dubai were enough), and I have rarely met anyone who regretted going on their travels. Our greatest disappointments are nearly always for what we haven't done – not for what we have done. And don't let the feeble excuse of work keep you back; remember the Haitian proverb: If work is such a good thing, how come the rich haven't grabbed it all for themselves?

Project work

Produce a piece of travel writing about your home city, town or region, or about any city, town or region you know well. You may choose any ONE of the following styles of presentation:

- an **account by a visitor** in the manner of Colin Thubron (page 87), Paul Theroux (page 175), Michael Palin (page 44) or Bill Bryson (pages 20–21, 39–43 and 109–110) in which:
  - the culture, customs and people are more important than the places of interest;
  - you offer observations and opinions which may be very personal, and may be sympathetic to, or critical of, the place you have chosen.
- a piece of **literary travel journalism**, in which you weigh the pros and cons of the area – its attractions, and its disadvantages (maybe even dangers!)
- a piece of **commercial travel journalism**, encouraging and enticing people to visit with a glowing account of the many attractions of the area.

You may present your work as any one of the following:

- an extract from a book
- a newspaper article or feature
- a website, or a design for one
- a TV documentary or travel show feature (on videotape or other recording format)
- a radio documentary or travel programme feature (on audiotape or other recording format)

Extract analysis

Which description below best describes the extract you have been reading? Complete the following:

Title of extract _____

Author _____

1 Text type: **a)** travel guide **b)** advertisement **c)** diary **d)** report **e)** autobiography

I think this extract is from a(n) _____ .

My reason for thinking this is that _____

_____ .

For example, on page _____, the author writes, '_____

_____'.

2 Language: **a)** informal **b)** formal

I think the language in this extract is _____ .

My reason for thinking this is that _____

_____ .

For example, on page _____, the author writes, '_____

_____'.

3 Tone: **a)** humorous **b)** serious **c)** critical

I think the tone of this extract is _____ .

My reason for thinking this is that _____

_____ .

For example, on page _____, the author writes, '_____

_____'.

4 Narrator: **a)** first person (I/we) **b)** second person (you/your) **c)** third person (he/she/they)

This extract is narrated in the _____ person.

For example, on page _____, the author writes, '_____
_____'.

5 Address: **a)** addresses the reader directly **b)** doesn't address the reader directly

In this extract, the writer _____ .

For example, on page _____, the author writes, '_____
_____'.

6 Period: **a)** up-to-date **b)** 20th century **c)** 19th century **d)** earlier than 19th century.

The period of this extract is _____ .

My reason for thinking this is that _____
_____ .

For example, on page _____, the author writes, '_____
_____'.

Extract analysis – example

Title of extract Barbados

Author Tradewinds Brochure

1 Text type: **a)** travel guide **b)** advertisement **c)** diary **d)** report **e)** autobiography

I think this extract is from a(n) **advertisement** .

My reason for thinking this is that **the extract is trying to persuade people to take a holiday in Barbados** .

For example, on page **62** , the author writes, '**A consistent favourite with British visitors, Barbados is an ideal introduction to the Caribbean** '.

2 Language: **a)** informal **b)** formal

I think the language in this extract is **informal** .

My reason for thinking this is that **the writer uses a style that is easy to read, friendly in tone and eager to please** .

For example, on page **63** , the author writes, ' **Beautiful beaches on her western shore are gently lapped by Caribbean waters** '.

3 Tone: **a)** humorous **b)** serious **c)** critical

I think the tone of this extract is **serious** .

My reason for thinking this is that **The extract is mostly concerned with using persuasion and giving information. It is not at all critical and there is very little humour** .

For example, on page **63** , the author writes, ' **Many of the hotels have a dress code in the evening. The hotels are generally quiet at night although some nights there may be a local band.** '.

4 Narrator: **a)** first person (I/we) **b)** second person (you/your) **c)** third person (he/she/they)

This extract is narrated in the **second** person.

For example, on page **63**, the author writes, '**there's an international atmosphere, with bars and restaurants to suit your every mood . . .**'.

5 Address: **a)** addresses the reader directly **b)** doesn't address the reader directly

In this extract, the writer **addresses the reader directly**.

For example, on page **62**, the author writes, '**Harrison's cave – where a special tram will take you down through an exciting cavern of stalagmites and stalactites**'.

6 Period: **a)** up-to-date **b)** 20th century **c)** 19th century **d)** earlier than 19th century.

The period of this extract is **20th century**.

My reason for thinking this is that **The style is modern and there are references to modern activities**.

For example, on page **62**, the author writes, '**. . . land-based facilities including championship golf and floodlit tennis**'.

Further Reading

Dangerous Journeys

Wind, Sand and Stars: Antoine de Saint-Exupéry, Penguin
The Wild Blue Yonder: The Picador Book of Aviation,
    Graham Coster, Picador
The Virago Book of Women Travellers, Virago Press
A Zoo in my Luggage: Gerald Durrell, Penguin
The Bafut Beagles: Gerald Durrell, Penguin
The Wind in my Wheels: Josie Dew, Warner
On Foot through Africa: Ffyona Campbell, Orion

The Great Outdoors

The Lost Continent and **Neither Here Nor There:** Bill Bryson,
    Secker & Warburg
A Walk in the Woods: Bill Bryson, Black Swan
Pole to Pole: Michael Palin, BBC Books
Full Circle: Michael Palin, BBC Books (*Around the World in
    80 Days* is available on BBC video)
The Real Beach – TV film first broadcast on Channel Four, on
    Saturday 12 February at 11.05 p.m. Compare with the
    'Land of Toys' section of Carlo Collodi's *Pinocchio* – read
    the book or hire the Walt Disney film version.

Cities

Sydney – The Rough Guide
Lonely Planet Guide to Sydney
One Day in the Life of Ivan Denisovich: Alexander
    Solzhenitsyn, Penguin
The Big Red Train Ride: Eric Newby, Picador
KGB: Yevgenia Albats, IB Tauris
London – The Rough Guide
The Lonely Planet Guide – Lebanon
Between Extremes: John McCarthy and Brian Keenan, Black
    Swan
Israel – The Rough Guide
Eyewitness Travel Guides – Paris: Dorling Kindersley

Roots

The Brendan Voyage: Tim Severin, Abacus
The Sinbad Voyage: Tim Severin, Abacus
The Jason Voyage: Tim Severin, Abacus
The *Kon Tiki* Expedition: Thor Hyerdahl, Flamingo
A Bend in the River: V S Naipaul, Penguin
North or South: Shiva Naipaul, Penguin
The Heart of the Hunter: Laurens van der Post, Penguin
A Story Like the Wind: Laurens van der Post, Penguin
A Far-Off Place: Laurens van der Post, Penguin
The Ascent of Everest: John Hunt, Mountaineers' Books
Into Thin Air: John Krakamer, Pan
K2 – The Story of the Savage Mountain: Jim Curran, Coronet

Strange lands

The Voyage of Maelduin *from* **A Book of Goblins:** ed. Alan
   Garner, Puffin
Gulliver's Travels: Jonathan Swift
The Voyage of the Dawn Treader: C.S. Lewis, Puffin
The Oxford Book of Exploration: Robin Hanbury-Tenison,
   Oxford University Press
The South Pole: Roald Amundsen
A Black Explorer at the North Pole: Matthew A. Henson,
   Bison Books
East is West: Freya Stark, Century Hutchinson
The Virago Book of Women Travellers: Virago Books
A Pattern of Islands: Arthur Grimble, John Murray
The Great Railway Bazaar: Paul Theroux, Penguin
The Old Patagonian Express: Paul Theroux, Penguin
Riding the Iron Rooster: Paul Theroux, Penguin
Lonely Planet Guides: the series includes several guides
   covering the islands of the Pacific
Space exploration: http://encarta.msn.com/events/world/space
NASA website: http://www.nasa.gov
British Interplanetary Society website:
   http://freespace.virgin.net/bis.bis/
Greenpeace website: http://www.greenpeace.org/

Acknowledgements

The Editor and Publishers would like to thank the following for permission to use copyright material:

Extract from 'Operation Raleigh: the start of an adventure' by John Blashford-Snell, published by HarperCollins Publishers. Reprinted by permission of HarperCollins Publishers Limited; Extracts from 'Holidays in Hell' by P. J. O'Rourke, published by Macmillan. Reprinted by permission of Macmillan, London; Extracts from 'Neither Here, Nor There' by Bill Bryson. © Bill Bryson. Published by Black Swan, a division of Transworld Publishers. All rights reserved. Reprinted by permission of Transworld Publishers; Extracts from 'Pickpockets and Thieves', taken from 'artoftravel.com'. Reprinted by permission of artoftravel.com; Extract from 'Notes From A Small Island' by Bill Bryson. © Bill Bryson. Published by Black Swan, a division of Transworld Publishers. All rights reserved. Reprinted by permission of Transworld Publishers; Extract from 'Around the World in 80 Days' by Michael Palin. Copyright © Michael Palin 1989. Reproduced by permission of BBC Worldwide Limited; Extract from 'Berner Oberland Magazine Summer 1999'. Reprinted by permission of Berner Oberland; Extract from 'Lonely Planet Guide to South India' Edition 1. published 1998. Reproduced by permission of Lonely Planet Publications; Extracts from 'Worldwide Holidays Brochure 2000' produced by Tradewinds Worldwide Holidays. Reproduced by permission of Tradewinds Worldwide Holidays; Extract from 'The Real Beach' by Dimitri Doganis. Reprinted by permission of the author; Extract from 'Sydney' by Jan Morris (Viking 1992) Copyright © Jan Morris, 1992. Reprinted by permission of Penguin Books Limited; Extract from 'Among the Russians' by Colin Thubron, published by William Heinemann. Reprinted by permission of Random House Group Limited; Extract from 'Travel Guide London' published by Dorling Kindersley. Reprinted with permission; Extract '48 Hours in Tel Aviv' by Mark Espiner, taken from 'The Guardian 13 November 1999' © Mark Espiner, first published in The Guardian. Reprinted by permission of The Guardian; Extract from 'Cities and Short Breaks brochure November 1999 – October 2000'. Reprinted by permission of Cresta Holidays, Altrincham; Extract from 'The Ghosts of Everest: The Authorised Story of the Search for Mallory and Irvine' by Jochen Hemmleb, Larry A. Johnson & Eric R. Simonson, first published in Great Britain by Macmillan in 1999. Copyright © 1999 by Jochen Hemmleb, Larry A. Johnson and Eric R. Simonson. Reproduced by permission of the authors c/o Rogers, Coleridge & White Limited, 20 Powis Mews, London W11 1JN in association with International Copyright Management, New York; Extract from 'The Jason Voyage' by Tim Severin, published by Random House. © Tim Severin 1983. Reprinted by permission of Sheil Land Associates Limited; Extract from 'An Area of Darkness' by V S Naipaul (Allen Lane 1968) Copyright © V S Naipaul 1968. Reprinted by permission of Penguin Books Limited; Extract from 'The Sorcerer's Apprentice' by Tahir Shah. Reprinted by permission of the Orion Publishing Group Limited; Extract from 'The Lost World of the Kalahari' by Laurens van der Post, published by Hogarth Press. Reprinted by permission of Random House Group Limited; Extracts from 'The Travels of Sir John Mandeville 1322' abridged by Denny & Filmer, published by HarperCollins Publishers. Reprinted with permission of HarperCollins Publishers Limited; Extract from 'Valley of the Assassins' by Freya Stark, published by John Murray (Publishers) Limited. Reprinted by permission of John Murray (Publishers) Limited; Extract from 'The Happy Isles of Oceania: Paddling the Pacific' by Paul Theroux (Hamish Hamilton 1992) Copyright © Cape Cod Scriveners Co. 1992. Reprinted by permission of Penguin Books Limited; Extract from 'On Another Planet' by George Monbiot, taken from 'The Guardian 13 November 1999 Copyright © George Monbiot, first published in the Guardian. Reprinted by permission of the Guardian.

The Publishers have made every effort to trace the copyright holders, but if they have inadvertently overlooked any, they will be pleased to make the necessary arrangements at the first opportunity.

ALSO IN

Heinemann
New Windmills

Founding Editors: Anne and Ian Serraillier

Chinua Achebe Things Fall Apart
David Almond Skellig
Maya Angelou I Know Why the Caged Bird Sings
Margaret Atwood The Handmaid's Tale
Jane Austen Pride and Prejudice
J G Ballard Empire of the Sun
Stan Barstow Joby; A Kind of Loving
Nina Bawden Carrie's War; Devil by the Sea; Kept in the Dark; The Finding; Humbug
Lesley Beake A Cageful of Butterflies
Malorie Blackman Tell Me No Lies; Words Last Forever
Ray Bradbury The Golden Apples of the Sun; The Illustrated Man
Betsy Byars The Midnight Fox; The Pinballs; The Not-Just-Anybody Family; The Eighteenth Emergency
Victor Canning The Runaways
Jane Leslie Conly Racso and the Rats of NIMH
Susan Cooper King of Shadows
Robert Cormier We All Fall Down; Heroes
Roald Dahl Danny, The Champion of the World; The Wonderful Story of Henry Sugar; George's Marvellous Medicine; The BFG; The Witches; Boy; Going Solo; Matilda; My Year
Anita Desai The Village by the Sea
Charles Dickens A Christmas Carol; Great Expectations; Hard Times; Oliver Twist; A Charles Dickens Selection
Berlie Doherty Granny was a Buffer Girl; Street Child
Roddy Doyle Paddy Clarke Ha Ha Ha
Anne Fine The Granny Project
Jamila Gavin The Wheel of Surya
Graham Greene The Third Man and The Fallen Idol; Brighton Rock
Thomas Hardy The Withered Arm and Other Wessex Tales
L P Hartley The Go-Between
Ernest Hemmingway The Old Man and the Sea; A Farewell to Arms
Barry Hines A Kestrel For A Knave
Nigel Hinton Getting Free; Buddy; Buddy's Song; Out of the Darkness
Anne Holm I Am David
Janni Howker Badger on the Barge; The Nature of the Beast; Martin Farrell

Pete Johnson The Protectors
Jennifer Johnston Shadows on Our Skin
Geraldine Kaye Comfort Herself
Daniel Keyes Flowers for Algernon
Dick King-Smith The Sheep-Pig
Elizabeth Laird Red Sky in the Morning; Kiss the Dust
D H Lawrence The Fox and The Virgin and the Gypsy; Selected Tales
George Layton The Swap
Harper Lee To Kill a Mockingbird
C Day Lewis The Otterbury Incident
Joan Lingard Across the Barricades; The File on Fraulein Berg
Penelope Lively The Ghost of Thomas Kempe
Jack London The Call of the Wild; White Fang
Bernard MacLaverty Cal; The Best of Bernard Mac Laverty
James Vance Marshall Walkabout
Ian McEwan The Daydreamer; A Child in Time
Michael Morpurgo My Friend Walter; The Wreck of the Zanzibar;
The War of Jenkins' Ear; Why the Whales Came; Arthur, High King
of Britain; Kensuke's Kingdom; Hereabout Hill
Beverley Naidoo No Turning Back
Bill Naughton The Goalkeeper's Revenge
New Windmill A Charles Dickens Selection
New Windmill Book of Classic Short Stories
New Windmill Book of Fiction and Non-fiction: Taking Off!
New Windmill Book of Haunting Tales
New Windmill Book of Humorous Stories: Don't Make Me Laugh
New Windmill Book of Nineteenth Century Short Stories
New Windmill Book of Non-fiction: Get Real!
New Windmill Book of Non-fiction: Real Lives, Real Times
New Windmill Book of Scottish Short Stories
New Windmill Book of Short Stories: Fast and Curious
New Windmill Book of Short Stories: From Beginning to End
New Windmill Book of Short Stories: Into the Unknown
New Windmill Book of Short Stories: Tales with a Twist
New Windmill Book of Short Stories: Trouble in Two Centuries
New Windmill Book of Short Stories: Ways with Words
New Windmill Book of Short Stories by Women
New Windmill Book of Stories from many Cultures and Traditions:
Fifty-Fifty Tutti-Frutti Chocolate-Chip
New Windmill Book of Stories from Many Genres: Myths, Murders
and Mysteries

How many have you read?